THE SHRINKING GODDESS

MINEKE SCHIPPER

THE
SHRINKING
GODDESS

*Power, Myth and the
Female Body*

The Westbourne Press

The Westbourne Press
Gable House, 18–24 Turnham Green Terrace, London w4 1QP
www.westbournepress.co.uk

Published 2024 by The Westbourne Press

ISBN 978 1 908906 59 5
eISBN 978 1 908906 60 1

Printed and bound by Thomson Press, India

CONTENTS

ILLUSTRATIONS

MAPS

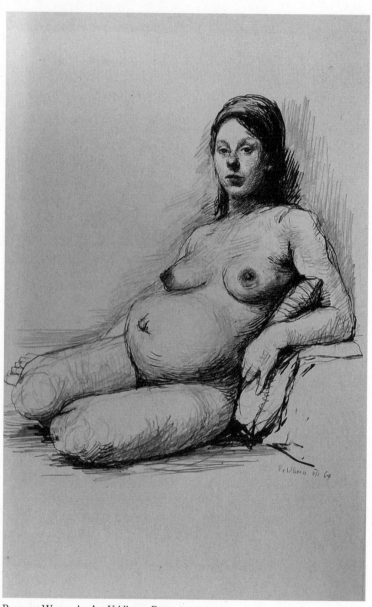

Pregnant Woman by Aat Veldhoen. Rotaprint, 1964.

A PRECARIOUS HOUSE OF STORIES

The eye is not satisfied with seeing, nor the ear filled with hearing.

Ecclesiastes 1:8

OVER THE PAST five decades I have researched proverbs, art, myths and other verbal genres that magnify the differences between men and women. These sources – many of which are thousands of years old – shed light on our conversations around gender today. For the most part, our myths are mainly concerned with justifying, or establishing, a patriarchal, hierarchical order. However, other genres, such as proverbs, art and folklore, struggle to address the precarious gender balance of power in society.

Comparing the cultural legacies of widely different people from around the globe, I discovered similar ideas and cultural messages – often with the same meaning and (mostly) similar form – expressed through different metaphors:

Women are like banana leaves: they never come to an
end in the plantation.
(Ganda, Uganda)

Women are like shoes, they can always be replaced.
(Rajasthani, India)

Women are like buses: if one leaves, another one will
come.
(Spanish, Venezuela)

Women are like frogs, for one diving into the water,
four others turn up to the surface.
(Spanish, Peru)

This is one of many examples. Such similarities cannot be due
only to globalisation, as they originate from times and cultures
without demonstrable contact. How is this possible? Our
common patterns as human beings have to do with the shape
and functions of the human body and its basic needs, such as
food, shelter, safety and procreation, and with emotions such as
fear, longing, joy and sorrow, experienced by us all.

I have always told my students: if you look only for differences,
you will find only differences. If you look for similarities, they are
in front of you. Instead of looking for what we share, conversations
around human identity are inclined to blow up our differences.
Today's global order goes back to a house of stories, built on
mythical foundations, by influential storytellers, who established
a strong belief in the differences between sexes.

Since the beginning of time, human beings have devised
images of themselves and embedded them in stories, songs and
other forms of artistic expression. The nature of how human

beings present themselves through such images has varied according to the interests of those involved and the contexts in which they lived. One of the main tasks of my field is to study the similarities and differences of how humankind presents itself in oral and written traditions.

Looking into the worldwide harvest of cultural legacies helps us to put our local views into a wider picture. To make sense of a patriarchal structure, and the ways in which it is sustained, we need to understand its foundations. This book takes a wide-ranging look at our global house of stories and ideas around gendered body parts and the power they wield. Awareness is a modest first, crucial step towards questioning our established views of the self and the other.

Humanity is divided by an ongoing history of exclusion, with devastating consequences. Nonetheless, small miracles happen. In spring 2004 I had a totally unexpected experience. After my book *Never Marry a Woman with Big Feet* came out, *The Times* invited me to write about the how and the why of this book. Titled 'Beware of women with big feet', the article went into my extensive travels and conversations with a large variety of people, first in Africa where I lived several years in DR Congo, later in other parts of the world. Following my travels, I spent years working on the collected material of more than 15,000 proverbs about women (and men), studying how proverbs have helped impose restrictions on women's place and role in contemporary society.[1]

Two weeks after this article appeared as the leading *Times Weekend Review* article, a huge, mysterious airmail package arrived for me on the doorstep of my Leiden University office. It contained a number of impressive books of Arabic proverbs and a letter from the generous Saudi sender, living in Riyadh. He

---

1   London: Yale University Press, 2004

had read my article and assured me in his letter that, had he been in Leiden, he would have loved to have had a long conversation. Instead, to express his appreciation for the article, he had sent me this gift. This encouraging gesture from the other side of the world convinced me that patient research may build cross-cultural bridges.

The power of myths

Myths deal with crucial issues that affect society. We are enmeshed in traditions passed down from generation to generation, which connect us more closely to our ancestors than we may realise. They lay the foundations for human existence. As long as people believe in their own stories, the established order depicted in their traditions persists.

In this book myths, proverbs, popular culture and past philosophical and medical perceptions tell a pregnant story that throws new light on the female body, with the help of illuminating pictures. Cultural traditions from around the world reveal a desperate need for control over 'her', leading to extraordinary beliefs and practices, from fanged wombs to the so-called island of menstruating men. Similar patterns make us ask to what extent the male wish for dominance over the female body has been successful.

The first part of this book goes back to the enormous impact of myths, even today. It shares a history of creation goddesses, and how they slowly and surely made way for male creators. Part II goes into the enlightening wealth of stories and comments on the mysteries of the female body, from the hospitable breasts praised as the 'hills of paradise' to fear of the hymen, and the awesome power of the womb's life-giving capacity.

In the third and final part of this book we are confronted with the consequences of globally developed hierarchies in human history: the continuing violence of physical power inspired mainly by mental insecurity and fear; the ongoing demonstrable preference for sons over daughters in many societies; and the vulnerability of those declared subordinates who risk ending up in contempt of their own appearance, thanks to compelling commercials and other influential media. Finding out how today's widely held views came into being, and what they tell us about society in the past and present, will help us in taking new roads into the future.

Myths explain how, over millennia, female power had to be curbed. This was done through stereotyping women as capricious, unjust and demanding. Myths justify the notion that men were better positioned – and able – to run the world. Men's theft of female power, also called the theft of 'women's secret', is a striking motif in several parts of the world.

A Gikuyu story I was told in Kenya describes how women were once in charge. They were cruel, ruthless, and ruled like tyrants. The men did everything for them – they hunted, worked the land, cooked, cared for the children (in some versions they even breastfed the babies) and protected their families against enemies. The women handed out orders and did nothing. But no matter how zealously the men did their best to meet the women's demands, they were exploited as slaves. The female rulers were never satisfied. No wonder the men resorted to a ruse: they agreed among themselves to impregnate all the women at the same time. And while the women were giving birth, their unjust regime was overthrown. 'The men created a new order and strengthened their grip on society. Since then, justice and peace have reigned in Gikuyu society.'

This story gives the impression that matriarchal power was superseded by patriarchy; but matriarchy has never actually existed as a societal order. The existence of matriarchies, societies in which women are dominant, has been certain feminists' stubborn wishful thinking. Convincing proof has never been found – though there are many (mostly negative or threatening) stories about societies that in the past consisted of women only, or in which women reigned.[2]

In his bestseller *Sapiens*, Yuval Noah Harari concludes that biology makes lots of things possible which culture then restricts or forbids. That male dominance has developed almost universally cannot be a coincidence, he says, but he is unable to explain *why* this hierarchy remains so widely in force today:

> Maybe males of the species Homo sapiens are characterized not by physical strength, aggressiveness and competitiveness, but rather by superior social skills and a greater tendency to cooperate. We just don't know.[3]

Disappointing, really. In spite of the claim in the subtitle of his book – *A Brief History of Humankind* – the author is blind to the revealing light that myths throw on the origins of gendered inequality.

---

2   Cynthia Ellen, *The Myth of Matriarchal Prehistory*. Boston: Beacon Press 2000. A few communities have been described in which women and men shared their power in several respects, for example, in Çatalhöyük in Anatolia, a matrilocal urban settlement from the late Stone Age (six or seven millennia old), where about 6,000 to 8,000 people lived, see *The Creation of Patriarchy* by Gerda Lerner, (Oxford UP, 1986) pp. 30–32. For further explanation and stories see also *In het Begin was er Niemand* ('*In the Beginning There Was No One*' by Mineke Schipper (Prometheus, 2010) pp. 171–75.

3   Yuval Noah Harari, *Sapiens* (Vintage, 2011) p. 178.

Myths devote a great deal of attention to the body, and link messages about sexual hierarchy in a community to origin stories about gods and the first people. Over time, the basic creative and life-giving functions of mythical goddesses have been taken over by gods imagined and addressed as males. Various deities are themselves more than one sex, or create for themselves supplementary bodily functions they missed for the purpose of creating life or to nurse their babies (the Hindu god Shiva did this, as we will see), something the monotheistic religions were keen to move away from. Many stories have been recast over time so that the male sex is elevated over the female, usually ignoring non-gendered and intersex humans. In some stories the new divine leader radically eliminates his primeval mother in a dramatic battle.

Thousands of years ago, the female capacity to produce life became associated with an uncontrollable nature that had to be tamed. Many myths tried to muzzle this frightening life force by introducing a reassuring male supreme god or ancestor as the creator of all life. In an Egyptian story, the primordial ocean god Nun bears the sun god Atum, and this second male creator subsequently copulates with his own hand. He masturbates and puts his semen in his mouth and, by spitting it out, he creates his children, Shu and Tefnut. In an ancient Egyptian tomb text, he manifests himself as an autonomous procreator:

Before heaven came into being,
Before earth came into being,
Before the ground and the reptiles had been created
    here.
I was the great one who came into being out of myself,
All alone I fulfilled all my desires,

I considered in my heart and planned in my head
How I would shape and create myriad forms.
So it was I who spat forth Shu and vomited up Tefnut.
This happened when I was still alone ...
I masturbated with my fist, I copulated with my
    hand,
I spat from my mouth, out of myself.[4]

In many traditions, a male god creates life by uttering a powerful word, or by using his own hands and mud, dust or other materials, including from his innermost body. An innate lack of male birth-giving power is transformed into success stories about a divine masculine order that overcomes and regulates female chaos.

※

Myths present a desired social order – for some. Most myths confirm an order in which men are in charge, even though they remain dependent on women for offspring. This dependence has not only led to control over female sexuality, but also to an ostentatious male need for compensation in political, cultural and religious terms, and to a striking propensity to territoriality – excluding women from positions in which gender differences are totally irrelevant. On top of mythology and popular culture, philosophers and theologians have frequently warned that the female body disrupts the prescribed order and causes disaster.

The bias of a male perspective was safeguarded in societies where any who were not men were not allowed to recite or comment in public on holy texts, myths, epics, sometimes even proverbs,

---

4   Free translation from Papyrus Bremner-Rind 26, 21–27, 1 Bibliotheca Aegyptica 3, Brussels 1933: 59–61 and other magic tomb texts referring to myths. With thanks to Egyptologist Jacco Dieleman for personal information.

stopping all those who did not have the required physical features from contributing to the shaping of traditions. In many cultures and religions, it is still only men who are permitted to engage with sacred texts or lead religious services.

The study of the female body

Male fascination with the physical anatomy that they do not have has always been great, not only in storytelling and other verbal genres, but also in artistic depiction of the female body, from statuettes to cartoons. Appraisals of women range from delight to insecurity, distrust and fear. Contact between the sexes has been complicated by male fear of the vulva – a place in which, in cautionary tales in many cultures, the desire to devour is said to lurk. The power of this primal gateway spurned the delusion that a man who looks at female genitals will be punished with children born blind.[5] This book is about those ambiguous feelings towards indispensable, coveted, reviled and envied female body parts.

Information from women about their own sex is rare before the twentieth century. No doubt women had ideas about their own bodies (and about those of men), but until recently their views have had little impact. The knowledge they had was either silently taken over by the other sex or dismissed as unprofessional.

In Europe, female doctors and midwives were excluded from medicine as a scientific profession. Some women, like the twelfth-century abbess Hildegard von Bingen, wrote authoritative medical texts in Latin. Nonetheless, women were barred from secondary

5   Michael L. Satlow, *Jewish Constructions of Nakedness. Journal of Biblical Literature* 116 (3) Fall 1997, pp.441–442.

education and the study of medicine and, therefore, from access to more respected forms of medical practice. As a result, women's medical knowledge has rarely been preserved in books.

An exception is Jane Sharp's *The Midwives Book, or The Whole Art of Midwifry Discovered* (1671), a medical handbook based on rich experience with the female body. Hardly any knowledge is available about Sharp, except the detail on the book's title page that she practised as a midwife for over thirty years. There were no guilds for female doctors or midwives. By the end of the sixteenth century, most medical acts were exclusively reserved for members of medical guilds, to which women had no access.[6]

Woman with Unborn Child. Jane Sharp, *The Midwives Book*, 1671.

With all that in mind, it is unsurprising that most of what has been said and written about the female body originates from male sources or has been coloured by male perspectives.

---

6   Margaret R. Miles, *A Complex Delight* (University of California Press, 2008), chapter 4.

Over the centuries, research on human society has been led by men. Research from the female perspective at local, national and global levels is relatively recent: we do not know what women were saying or thinking among themselves, they wrote relatively little, and their own oral traditions have attracted interest only since the 1970s.

Moreover, in the cultures where they did their fieldwork, those male researchers often only had access to men. Thus, any subjects who were not male were reduced to 'muted groups'. This term was coined by Edwin Ardener, who concluded that in the social sciences there is an enormous discrepancy in knowledge about men and women: 'There is a real imbalance. We are, for practical purposes, in a male world. The study of women is on a level little higher than the study of the ducks and fowls they commonly own – a mere bird-watching indeed.'[7]

Meanwhile, whatever attention the female body did not receive in a professional, scientific capacity, it received in art. This Latin medieval student song explores an undulating feminine landscape:

> Softly shines her virgin bosom, And the breasts that
>   gently rise like the hills of Paradise.
> Oh, the joys of this possessing! [...]
> From her tender breasts decline, In a gradual
>   curving line,
> Flanks like swansdown white and fine. [...]
> 'Neath the waist her belly turneth Unto fulness, where
>   below
> In Love's garden lilies blow. Oh, the joys of this
>   possessing![8]

---

7   Edwin Ardener in: *Perceiving Women*, (Shirley Ardener, ed.) (Malaby Press, 1977) pp. 1–2.
8   'Flora' in *Wine, Women, and Song: Medieval Latin Students' Songs* (King's Classics, 1840) pp. 112–13.

In the twenty-first century, male students and rappers still sing about girls' bodies as property; however, in Western culture today, some such songs are strikingly violent. Bragging about one's potency conceals the fear of one's personal performances in 'Te lam Om te Zingen' ('Too Blotto to Sing'), a recent song popular in Utrecht University's Earth Sciences student union: 'My sledgehammer is my third leg / It rams rocks to pieces / but I'd rather shove it in your cave.' The girl submitted to this ramming finds it 'a bit strange', because she is only fourteen. The greater the male insecurity, the younger and less experienced the girls that are targeted.

The established order

Even though both sexes are needed for procreation, from ancient times onwards most societies selected only one sex for preferential treatment. In the case of newlyweds, only one of the families decided where the couple would live: with the family of the groom (patrilocal) or with the family of the bride (matrilocal). In cultures where hunting and gathering were replaced by large-scale agriculture, family relations began to move from matrilocal to patrilocal residence, and more and more often young women had to put up with the man's family instead of the other way round.[9] The young women ended up in unfamiliar surroundings, under supervision of and submitting to the rules of the 'others', whereas the husband had the comfort of staying with his kinfolk on the family compound. Mothers-in-law and daughters-in-law are commonly presented as being suspicious of or even hostile towards each other.

---

9   Ruth H. Munroe, Robert L. Carol R. Ember and Melvin Ember, 'The Conditions Favoring Matrilocal Versus Patrilocal Residence', *American Anthropologist* 73 (1971), pp. 571–94.

In many cultures, girls are considered to be 'in transit' in their own homes. Indeed daughters, destined to depart, are considered 'spilt water' (Chinese) or 'cigarette ashes' (Arabic). Children come to belong to the clan of the husband, whereas their mothers never entirely belong anywhere. Or in the words of a Luba proverb: 'A daughter is like a raindrop, she will fertilise the fields of others.'

Because women have often been considered male possessions, rape has been seen not so much as a violation of a woman's honour, but as a defilement of her owner's property. In the case of an unmarried girl, her rapist would pay compensation to the original 'owner', her father, and the victim was passed into the hands of the rapist, her new 'owner'. This arrangement is outlined in the Book of Deuteronomy (22:28–29) in the Hebrew Bible, and, in many societies, it is still a common course of events.

Fathers exercise authority in patriarchal societies. The term patriarchy consists of the Greek words *pater* ('father') and *archè* ('beginning' or 'reigning principle'). The establishment of patriarchal relations was a long process that took place at different moments in different parts of the world. In the Middle East this development took place over 2,500 years (about 3100–600 BCE). The oldest known laws are engraved in clay tablets dug up in Mesopotamia (now Iraq). Inscriptions in cuneiform characters make clear that sexuality and female birth-giving capacity were controlled by men very early, as the women's history author Gerda Lerner convincingly demonstrates in *The Creation of Patriarchy*.[10]

Thanks to the inscriptions on clay tablets from the earliest known period (c. 3000 BCE) we know that women actively participated in economic, religious and political life, but depended on a man for their position in society. Wherever

10   Here I gratefully refer to her chapter 1: 'Origins'. (OUP, 1986).

male dominance was established, an iron rule was that women who no longer pleased their menfolk lost their power. Men had their own home, whereas women belonged to men who had acquired rights over them. Women's place in the hierarchy was determined by the status of the men on whom they depended: their fathers, brothers and husbands.

All women had to accept, as given, the control of their sexuality and their reproductive processes by men or male-dominated institutions.[11]

Male control over the female body is still openly practised today. An eloquent example is the Taliban's immediate rebranding of the Women's Affairs Ministry back to the Ministry for Propagation of Virtue and Prevention of Vice, soon after regaining power in Afghanistan in August 2021.

Power generates fear – the fear of losing one's acquired power. The fact that men are dependent on women for their children upset the balance between the sexes from the very start, creating a strong male desire for compensation and the need for power and control over women's bodies. This book is heavily weighted towards myths propagated by men about the female body – often insinuating its weakness. Where myths that extol the power of the woman and goddess still survive, in whole or parts, they are precious and indicative perhaps that before the whispers of centuries distorted them, there were more stories about female empowerment. Regardless, the sheer quantity and depth of sources by men exerting control over the female body is, itself, testament to its indisputable indispensability. Without female resistance, male fear of and need to control the female anatomy would be unnecessary. After all, why should you be afraid of someone who is insignificant?

---

11   *Ibid.* p.100.

PART I

FROM FEMALE TO MALE CREATORS

Cycladic marble female figures; the one at the centre is pregnant. Archaeological Museum, Athens. Syros, 2800–2300 BCE.

CHAPTER ONE

MOTHERS OF ALL LIFE

To the Mother of the Gods
Divine are your honours, O mother of the gods and
nurturer of all,
Yoke your swift chariot drawn by bull-slaying lions
And, O mighty goddess who brings things to pass,
join our prayers.
Many named and revered, you are queen of the sky,
For in the cosmos yours is the throne in the
middle, because
The earth is yours and you give gentle nourishment
to mortals
Gods and men were born of you.[1]

MODELS OF WOMEN DATE BACK to the earliest signs of
civilization. Such statues certainly predate the oldest written
prayers. These figures were usually carved in stone, bone or ivory,
with prominent breasts, bellies and vulvas. Dating between 10,000

---

[1] 'To the Mother of the Gods,' in: Orphic Hymns: Text and Translation by Apostolos
N. Athanassakis. The next oldest is the Venus of Willendorf, at around 30,000 years
old.

to 20,000 years old, they have been found in many places, from Europe to East Asia. In 2008 a small ivory figure was unearthed in six fragments in a hollow rock in southwest Germany, a statuette with strikingly big breasts and a marked vulva, carved from a mammoth tusk. This so-called Venus of Hohle Fels – almost 6 cm high and between 35,000 and 40,000 years old – is the most ancient so far discovered in a series of mother images that archaeologists call Venuses. The next oldest is the Venus of Willendorf, at around 30,000 years old.

Venus of Hohle Fels.
Blaubeuren Museum of Prehistory, Germany.

Venus of Willendorf.
Museum of Natural History, Vienna.

'Venus' is a problematic anachronism for these female figures, because Venus, the goddess of love, arrived considerably later. She is just one of many Roman goddesses, ranked below a supreme reigning Father God. The term 'protecting mother figure' or 'fertility symbol' seems more appropriate here:

Looking back so many thousands of years later at these earliest figures, it seems as if humanity's first image of life was the Mother. [...] Images of giving birth, offering nourishment from the breast and receiving the dead back into the womb for rebirth occur in the Palaeolithic as they do 10,000 years later in the Neolithic and 5,000 years after that in the Bronze and Iron Ages – and, indeed, are present to this day in Western culture in the rituals surrounding the Virgin Mary. It is not surprising that these images of the goddess appear throughout human history, for they all express a similar vision of life on Earth, one where the creative source of life is conceived in the image of a Mother and where humanity feels itself and the rest of creation to be the Mother's children.[2]

The divine breast never dries

The mother figure has been placed on a pedestal around the world for tens of thousands of years. In the words of an English proverb: 'God could not be everywhere, that's why He created mothers.' Sometimes, it feels as if the mother figure is the divine presence herself. The breast is a significant part of the mother figure, and the earthly breast is no less cherished than the heavenly. This is true for cultures around the world, for example in this Spanish proverb: 'My home is my mother's breast', and this contemporary Chinese poem, which sighs yearningly:

---

2   Anne Baring and Jules Cashford. The Myth of the Goddess (Arkana Penguin Books, 1993) pp. 9–10.

Mother, my mother
Hold me tight in your warm embrace
Because the dark night is imminent.[3]

'The earth, our mother, feeds us, waters us and clothes us' is a
Russian saying. In the same way that some origin stories lengthen
the first penis to such extreme dimensions that the owner has to
wrap it around his middle to be able to walk unhindered, the
breasts of goddesses in origin stories grow to unlikely dimensions.
Some stories about the pre-Islamic Arab goddess al-Uzza say
that her breasts were so huge that she would throw them over
her shoulders to let them hang down her back.[4] Sometimes, the
breasts of goddesses even gain special powers.

The breasts of the Greek goddess Hera were so powerful
that they left their mark on our galaxy. As the myth goes, Hera's
husband, the supreme god Zeus, was so fond of Hercules, his
son by a mortal lover, that he wanted to immortalise him. So
he placed the baby at the breasts of his sleeping spouse Hera to
suckle. The baby sucked so hard at Hera's nipples that she woke
up and realising this was not her own child, she angrily pushed
him off, causing her divine milk to squirt high into the air, where
it continues to brighten the Milky Way. The incident inspired
fine artists such as Rubens, many centuries later.

---

3   Quoted by poet and minister Jidi Majia, at a conference I attended in Xining,
     Western China in the summer of 2011.
4   Aicha Rahmouni, Storytelling in Chefchaouen Northern Morocco (Brill, 2014)
     p.60.

Peter Paul Rubens, Birth of the Milky Way, 1636–1637.

A dry human breast was seen as a curse, but Mother Goddesses blessed mortals with their abundantly nourishing breasts:

> The mother as breast is the Alma Mater, the Mother of Corn in ancient Greece and Asia and the Americas and, where agriculture was unknown, the Old Woman of the Seals of the Eskimo, the mother of Walruses of the Chukchi.[5]

On Babylonian clay tablets dating back millennia, the Alma Mater is known as 'The Mother with the faithful breast' or 'She whose breasts never failed'. Breasts were sometimes depicted in stylised spirals or circles, impressively emphasised, or even

---

5   Wolfgang Lederer, *Fear of Women*, (Harcourt Brace Jovanovich, 1968) p. 122.

multiplied as in the case of Artemis, also referred to as Diana of Ephesus. Stories tell how milk or honey, blood or wine – or in an Inuit story, fish – flowed from Artemis's nipples.[6]

Creation goddesses

The shamanistic goddess Xiwangmu ('Queen Mother of the West') is one of the oldest Chinese deities. The first inscription referring to her is found on an oracle bone from around 1600 BCE. In ancient times, the Chinese side of the Himalayas known as the Kunlun Mountains were considered a paradise where the immortals were supposed to live, including Mother Xiwangmu. Nobody knew Xiwangmu's beginning or end,[7] but her dazzling beauty was glorified by poets. According to local tradition, Xiwangmu is the one the Bible refers to as the Queen of Sheba, who went to visit King Solomon and gave birth to his son Menelik, to whom she would hand over the throne of her earthly realm.

In the Kunlun Mountains, Xiwangmu attained a high state of spiritual enlightenment, and there she still reigns over the cosmic powers thanks to her peach tree, which stands as the axis between Heaven and Earth and bears the fruits of immortality. The peaches ripen only once every thousand years and at these rare moments the other gods join Xiwangmu in a heavenly banquet. If a human succeeds in eating one of those peaches, they will be blessed with miraculous longevity.

---

6   *Ibid.* 14ff.
7   According to the Taoist writer Zhuangzi (fourth century BCE).

Xiwangmu, Golden Mother/First Ruler/Queen Mother of the West. Eastern Han Dynasty. Pottery, 200 CE.

Xiwangmu Statue in Western China, honoured with rainbow-coloured fireworks. Mother's Day, date unknown.

Coatlicue, the Aztec goddess of
the earth – 'our grandmother'.
National Anthropological
Museum, Mexico City, ca. 1500.

According to the stories, Xiwangmu always wears a rainbow-
coloured dress with winged sleeves. She helps, protects, gives
excellent advice and takes care of humanity's elixir of life, nurturing
her favourites.[8] She continues to be ceremonially worshipped, as I
found out some years ago when attending a Mother's Day festival
in the countryside near the city of Xining, where many people
gathered in her honour.

Many disparate cultures, despite having little or no contact
with one another, have similar stories about a powerful goddess
who manifests herself in all the living earth, water and air. The
earth is her body, stretching out to the horizon, and all that exists
belongs to her. In these origin stories not only plants, trees and
animals came up from her birth canals, but also the first human

---

8   Dashu, Max, *Xi Wangmu, the shamanic great goddess of China* (Supressed Histories
     Archive, accessed online October 2023).

beings: 'The little people crawled out in the dark like grasshoppers, their bodies naked and soft. Their eyes were closed; they hadn't opened them yet.' (Acoma Pueblo, New Mexico.)[9]

Usually, oral storytelling has no reliable dates; oral traditions are transmitted from one generation to the next and they change along with the political, religious and cultural circumstances of the day. In some myths, when life ends, this mighty mother figure takes everything back into her hospitable womb. An example from the Middle East makes clear that worldviews were changing. In some stories about the creation of Adam, the Earth is extremely worried about what is going to happen to her bodily material used for the creation of the first human body. In several Hebrew and Arabic variants, the Earth has already lost control over it. God instructs the Angel Gabriel to collect dust from the four corners of the Earth, but the Earth refuses to relinquish any of her precious body. The same happens to other heavenly messengers sent down in vain. The Earth fears that humankind is gradually going to destroy her beauty. In one Jewish story, God Himself must stretch out His own arms to dig up the required dust, while the Earth loudly protests. She is especially concerned because she foresees that some of the creatures made from her own body will end up in Hell. The very thought makes her burst into tears, her face changing into a landscape full of springs. In an Arabic story, Allah comforts the Earth with a solid promise: 'what has been taken from you, shall be returned to you.'[10] And indeed, this is the human fate: the Earth will take all of us back.

In several stories, the Mother Goddess gives birth to and nourishes all life without any intervention or contribution from

---

9   Marta Weigle, *Creation and Procreation* (University of Pennsylvania Press, 1982) p. 46.

10   Abdullah Al-Udhari, *The Arab Creation Myth* (Prague: Archangel, 1997) pp. 136–138.

a male god: everything comes forth from this generous female body, as in some Native American narratives:

> The mother of our songs, the mother of our seed, bore us in the beginning of things and she is the mother of all types of men, the mother of all nations. She is the mother of the thunder, the mother of the streams, the mother of the trees and of all things. She is the mother of the world and of the older brothers, the stone-people. She is the mother of the fruits of the earth and of all things. She is the mother of our youngest brothers, the French and the strangers. She is the only mother we possess. (Kagaba, Colombia)[11]

In some Chinese stories, instead of giving birth to them, the goddess Nüwa creates the first people with her own hands, without male intervention:

> This is what people tell: when heaven and earth had been created, there were no human beings yet. Nüwa, the primeval goddess, wandered through the quiet world and the silence filled her body with loneliness. Near a spring she found yellow soil, picked some up and began to mould a creature like herself. When she put it down beside the spring the creature began to laugh. Nüwa enjoyed the sound of laughing so much that she made another one, and still another one, and many more, shaping each of them carefully and beautifully with her hands. [...] She placed them on the earth. They all laughed and danced

---

11   Konrad Preuss in Weigle, *Spiders & Spinsters: Women and Mythology* (University of New Mexico Press, 1982) pp. 45–46.

and enjoyed themselves, and Nüwa called them her sons
and daughters. (Han, China)[12]

In later versions Nüwa lost her creative independence to become
the sister and/or wife of Fuxi – and they were represented together
with a human upper body and an underbody in the form of two
intertwined snakes.

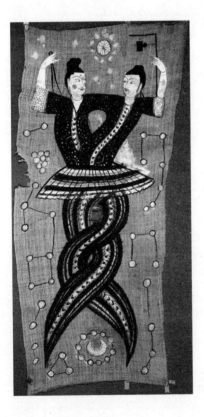

Nüwa and Fuxi. Silk painting,
Xinjiang Uighur Autonomous Region
Museum, Xinjiang. Mid eighth
century.

12   Lihui Yang and Deming An, *Handbook of Chinese Mythology*, (OUP, 2009) pp. 170–
     172; Yuan Ke 1993 p. 4; Mathieu, Rémi, 'Étude sur la mythologie et l'ethnologie de la
     Chine ancienne', Traduction annotée du Shanhai jing, (College de France, Institut
     des Hautes Éudes Chinoises, 1983) p. 63.

In Chinese, the key concept 'god' originally meant 'the ability to bear children'. Traces of Nüwa's early independence are still detectable in ancient myths,[13] but during the course of history, the idea of 'bringing forth' completely disappeared from the ancient meaning, and in Chinese myths – no less than in other parts of the world – the Mother Goddess ended up in a submissive role as the partner of a male god, or she herself changed into a male character. Indeed, in many creation myths around the world, the mother figure gradually undergoes metamorphosis. Either she becomes petrified, or she no longer fulfils her creative tasks, her sex changes or someone snatches her creative powers:

> We can no longer see her in the way we can see a person, even though she has legs and arms, a head, a heart, flesh, bones, and blood. Her flesh is the soil now; her hair has become trees and vegetation; her bones are the rocks, and her breath is the wind. As she lies there, spread out, we live on her. When she moves, there is an earthquake.[14]

In some variants of these creation myths, everything takes an abrupt turn when a new character, Old Man, is introduced. Old Man sits down upon the mother's body and, without further comment, begins to transform her – he pulls bits from her flesh and rolls them into tiny balls. The last balls look 'different from any of the preceding ones. He called them men and they looked

13   cf. Ye Shuxian, oral information as an example of China's creation and origin myths; (2011). See Bret Hinsch 'Prehistoric Images of Women from North China Region: The Origins of Chinese Goddess Worship?' *Journal of Chinese Religions*, 32.1 (2004) 47–82; and Robert H. Lowie, *Primitive Religion*, (Liveright Publishing, 1925) p.77, p. 275.

14   Franz Boas, James Alexander Teit, Livingston Farrand, Marian K. Gould, Herbert Joseph Spinden. *Folk-tales of Salishan and Sahaptin Tribes*, (American Folklore Society, 1969) p. 80.

like Indians, and when he blew on them, they became alive.'[15] In these myths it is Old Man, not the immortal mother, who creates human beings.

The creator is not always explicitly gendered as male or female. There are some examples of a non-gendered creation god, for example in this myth which has survived in Barua: 1–2:

> In the beginning there were no gods and no people. The water of the ocean embraced the void. Earth and heaven did not exist yet, there was no air yet, there were no animals, no rulers, no countries and no living beings yet. Nor did the sun, the moon and the stars exist. There was neither earth nor heaven.

There was only one omnipotent being, the Great God who remained suspended in the sky like a swarm of bees in a hive.

Specific dates for most oral traditions are unreliable, so it is hard to say exactly when the gender of creators first started to mutate from female to male. But as the myths developed through the ages, the creation of life almost everywhere moved away from the earlier ideas of an independent, birth-giving and nourishing Mother Goddess.[16]

Farming and fertility

Researchers generally agree that early agriculture was invented by women, whose task was to collect seeds, fruits and eggs while

---

15   *Ibid.*

16   e.g., Baring and Cashford, 1991; Lerner, *The Creation of Patriarchy*, 1986; Graves and Patai, *Hebrew Myths*, (Anchor Books/Doubleday, 1964) p. 26; David Leeming, *Myth. A Biography of Belief* (Oxford University Press, 2002) pp. 41, 79.

men went hunting. These women noticed that seeds or parts of tubers that fell to the ground germinated on their own, so they began to plant seeds and root vegetables around the cave or hut where they lived. Aside from the sowing and harvesting of crops, utilising healing herbs, learning how to bake bread, creating clay pots for ritual and household use and weaving and dyeing clothes are some of the earliest discoveries that have been attributed to women.[17]

After the invention of agriculture, women began to grow food near their homes. Thanks to their increasing provision to food stores, the prestige of women increased, especially when the hunting men came home empty-handed – a situation that no doubt led to tensions.

Thanks to agriculture, people became more aware of their own situation. In so far as hunting was a sacred activity, so was farming surrounded by rituals and ceremony. People looked with religious awe upon the hidden forces of the earth that brought forth all creatures, plants, animals and humans. Most agricultural activities were projected onto the particular powers of a goddess. The earth as the nourishing mother of life was considered full of magic power, bridging the visible and the invisible order.

In order to guarantee a successful harvest, sacrifices were made. Usually, the first corn was left standing in the field and the first fruits were left on the trees as a gesture of restitution. There were sacrifices of animals or humans, as a means of recycling holy energy.

Human sexuality became more and more connected to the divine power that fertilised the earth. In Neolithic mythology, the harvest was seen as the fruit of a sacred marriage. The rain united

---

17   Sierksma, *De roof van het vrouwengeheim* (Den Haag: Mouten & Co 1962), chapter 9.

Heaven and Earth: the female soil united with the male semen raining down from the sky. In various cultures, people had ritual sex when planting their crops. Imitating the harvest as a fruit of the sacred marriage between Heaven and Earth was performed as a sacred act 'to activate the creative energies of the soil, just as the farmers spade or plough also opens the womb of the earth and made it big with seed.' In ancient Israel such customs provoked the anger of various prophets such as Ezekhiel, who did not condone the ceremonies in honour of Asherah, a very popular fertility Canaanite goddess.[18] Through the generation and regeneration of crops, there developed a belief that dying and coming back to life were inextricably linked. It was believed that irreparable disasters would take place if no sacrificial blood was shed in honour of the eternal cycle. The Mother Goddess, though still considered loving and generous, began to change into a rather capricious, even cruel, being, because of the sacrifices she was believed to demand from her children to ensure a successful harvest.

Cybele, a widely worshipped fertility goddess, is a prime example. Most likely her foremother was a local Anatolian Mother Goddess, a precursor found in the earliest settlements of Çatalhöyük, where various images of plump women have been dug up. Physical birth-giving was a weighty topic in the Çatalhöyük sanctuaries of Anatolia (around 7500–5700 BCE). Archaeologists found giant stone reliefs of impressive female figures with huge breasts, bellies and thighs; left and right of the throne, their arms resting on a leopard or lioness. They are flanked by the horns of a bull or skulls of wild pigs – remains of successful hunting. These Stone Age images may well have been appropriated in later manifestations of Cybele and the Greek goddesses Artemis and Demeter.

---

18   Karen Armstrong, *A Short History of Myth* (Canongate, 2005) p. 43.

Hunting was a male activity, but the god of hunting was often female and the gods of agriculture were originally female too. Artemis was mistress of the animals as well as the source of life. The hunters who risked their lives in order to keep their wives and children alive understood that women were the source of new life. They were the ones who guaranteed continuity of the group, while men were replaceable.[19] Depictions of Cybele, the Great Goddess of Anatolia with a lion in her lap or on a chariot pulled by lions and leopards, are certainly reminiscent of the much older Neolithic stone reliefs found in Çatalhöyük.

Anatolian goddess with a newborn baby, flanked by lionesses, Çatalhöyü. Museum of Anatolian Civilizations, Ankara, *c.* 6000–5500 BC

---

19   Karen Armstrong, *A Short History of Myth* (Canongate, 2005) Chapter 2.

For centuries, certain stories testified that Cybele's lover Attis was also her son. According to some myths, Cybele drove Attis insane with jealousy, while in other versions he killed himself because she no longer reciprocated his love. Whatever the cause, and regardless of whether Attis was a simple shepherd or god of fertility, Attis castrated himself and bled to death, and from his blood sprang the first violets. After his death, a ritual was performed during which Cybele brought Attis back to life. This is the origin of the popular ancient Cybele cult, which spread from Anatolia to Greece, Rome and many other places.

Inspired by Attis' example, all those who served Cybele as her priests were eunuchs. In Rome, where they were called Galli, they dressed in women's clothes, 'mostly yellow in colour, and a sort of turban, together with pendants and earrings, they also wore their hair long and bleached, and wore heavy make-up.'[20] After an ecstatic spring celebration on the 'Day of Blood', during which they mourned Attis, the priests castrated themselves. Running around, messy and disordered, they threw their testicles haphazardly into the houses they passed, a gesture the inhabitants appreciated as a special benediction.

This cult of the Mother Goddess with a son/lover was popular among many believers in the region, from the sixth century BCE till the end of the fifth century CE – the end of the Roman Empire. Like other great goddesses, Cybele protected fertility and the dead, as much as untamed nature and the animals. For Lucretius (99–55 BCE), Cybele as Magna Mater symbolises 'the world order'. Her image signifies the Earth, she is the mother of all, and the yoked lions that draw her chariot show the offspring's

---

20   For collected sources, see the Wikipedia entry for 'Galli'. The earliest surviving references to the galli come from the Greek Anthology, a tenth-century compilation of earlier material, where several epigrams mention or clearly allude to their castrated state.

duty of obedience to the parent. She herself is uncreated and thus essentially separate from and independent of her creations.[21]

Gradually myths were permeated with violence – believers thought the goddess provided them with food, but they felt that the harvest would come to nothing if no male had been sacrificed to the Mother Goddess. Those consorts were, in the words of Karen Armstrong, 'torn apart, dismembered, brutally mutilated, and killed before they can rise again, with the crops, to new life.'[22]

As agricultural practices became widespread, the powerful, loving goddess turned into a demanding one who needed, selfishly, bloodshed and the immolation of men and animals. From the anxious belief that the goddess would punish those who did not comply with the required sacrifices, terms such as demanding, irreconcilable and vengeful were applied to this goddess over the image of nurturing, motherly love.

From the creation of humankind to the invention of glass ceilings

There is a common thread throughout mythology whereby procreation – creating life by giving birth – was transformed into fabrication: creation from nothing, by word or gesture, or creation from everyday earthly materials by hand. In a Hrusso myth, the sky god takes the initiative from an earlier Earth Goddess who had previously procreated alone. Her power crumbles away and she is ordered to shrink:

---

21   For collected sources, see the Wikipedia entry for 'Cybele'. The Greek historian
      Strabo (c. 64 BCE–23CE) wrote about the sexual implications of Cybele's veneration.
22   Armstrong, 2005 pp. 49–50.

The Earth was too big for the Sky to hold in his arms. 'Though you are my wife,' he said, 'you are greater than I. How can I take you? Make yourself smaller.' The Earth complied, and thanks to her adaptability the mountains and valleys came into being. The Earth became small and the Sky was able to go to her in love. From their lovemaking every kind of tree and grass and all living creatures came into being. (Hrusso, India)[23]

Mother Earth had to make way for an almighty Father God. In the human world the small look up to the big, the young respect their elders, the weak bow down to the mighty. Today, most men conform to this when finding a wife, consciously or subconsciously obeying traditional proverbs warning those who are courting to look for a woman who is 'inferior' in stature, age or education. 'A woman without talents is already doing very well' is a well-worn saying in China. This message is echoed from Africa to Asia and the Americas in the warning, 'Never marry a woman with bigger feet than your own'.[24]

The supreme power of the goddess is to be found in early images and myths revering female fertility in various forms, from snake to sea to moon to virgin goddesses. The original key to the mystery of life was femininity, whether modelled on a human form or other. Originally Mother Earth had all the potential for stepping up to the echelon of Supreme Goddess, but her career was blocked by the glass ceiling of her sacred marriage with Heaven.

The male invention of the plough and the taming of oxen and other animals to draw it through the soil brought a new balance

---

23   Elwin, 1958 pp. 15–16.
24   I adapted this proverb for the title of my collection of proverbs about women from around the world, *Never Marry a Woman with Big Feet* (Speaking Tiger, 2004).

between male and female contributions. Economically speaking, male plough agriculture was superior to the older corn and tuber cultures invented by women, producing a much more considerable harvest. More people stayed alive longer, more children were born and small villages grew into bigger ones.[25]

From around 4000 BCE people began to build cities with fortified walls. Increasing male self-confidence inspired myths in which the creative role of goddesses was transferred to male gods and the first-born male, and those new stories served as the cement to bind society together. Life creation myths continued to occupy a crucial place in traditional stories, but the tenor of the stories changed.

In these mutated myths about the creation of humans, a male god creates. This male god also creates the first man before he creates the first woman. In addition, the first woman is often created from lower-quality materials than the first man. Three examples:

Hinegba took some earth and made man out of it. He then took some more earth and made woman out of it. Man is physically stronger than woman because he was created first, that is before the strength of the earth had been sapped by the creation of an earlier human being out of it. (Kwotto, Nigeria)[26]

The Lord of Heaven decided to fashion first ten men and then ten women out of the flesh and bones of fowls. As soon as he began working on the women he

25   Sierksma, 1962 p. 152.
26   Kwotto: J.R. Wilson. 'Ethnological Notes on the Kwottos of Toto (Panda) District, Keffi Division, Benue Province, Northern Nigeria.' *Journal of the African Society* XXXVII (1927–1928), p. 145.

ran out of material, and had to take clay instead. As a result, the women created had no strength and were too weak to labour. The Lord of Heaven then infused strength into their bodies. However, the women now became so powerful that the men were no match for them. Considering this to be unsuitable, the Lord took back half of their strength. (Oroqen, China)[27]

Aware of Adam's loneliness God created the first woman out of dust. Her name was Lilith. However, he had not used pure dust but filth and sediment instead. (Jewish Apocrypha)[28]

In many creation stories, a male Supreme Being first creates a complete man, then he brings a female human into being second. One could infer that woman is not necessarily an inferior being on account of being created second. On the contrary, a second creative effort could be better than the first, thanks to addressing errors encountered and overcome in the original model. However, appearing second came to be equated with 'less valuable'. This is in part because the male Supreme Being makes the first woman out of an insignificant body part of the first man, for example from his toe, rib or thumb. In some cases, the male Supreme Being urges the first man to make himself a wife, either from his own urine, sperm, foreskin or from a piece of flesh from his thigh. These small details all indicate such blatant sexual hierarchy that the messaging cannot be considered accidental.[29]

27   With thanks to Ye Shuxian who generously shared with me his unpublished collection of myths, p. 6: Narrator: Meng Xingquan; recorded by Meng Shuzhen.
28   Louis Ginzburg, *The Legends of the Jews*. Trans. Henrietta Szold. Philadelphia: 1967–1969. p. 65.
29   More details in *In het Begin was er Niemand*, Chapter 6.

How Eve lost her life-creating status

The story of the first ancestral couple in Judaism, Christianity and Islam is one of the best-known origin myths. Verbal and visual variants of the Adam and Eve story have spread globally – from Scandinavia to South Africa, from Mexico to Southeast Asia.

In the first book of the Bible, the first human being is created in God's image and likeness. Originally it is just a 'mud creature', shaped from *ha-adamah*, the earth, as a piece of pottery. The separation of the original being turns the two parts into gendered humans. Some scholars have argued that the name of Eve (in Hebrew, *Havah*) is close to *Yahweh*, the name of God: 'The potential of procreation justifies that closeness. […] Eve was not born from the first man, but split off from the first creature, bi-sexual, as the first part of the story says: he created the human in his image and likeness – man and woman he created them (plural).'[30] Moreover, Eve is described as 'the mother of all the living'.

In the most popular translation and interpretation of the next part of the story (Genesis 2), God creates Eve out of a rib from Adam's body. Eve is 'a help fit for' Adam, establishing Eve's inferiority, which was passed onto all women after her and serves as a justification of sexual hierarchy practices in Judaism, Christianity and Islam. Some researchers have stated that the translation of 'rib' from the Hebrew 'צלע' (*tzela*) is not correct in this context. The bone that became Eve was no rib, but a *baculum* or 'penis bone', a part some animals (including lions, chimpanzees and gorillas) still possess. After Adam had to sacrifice his *baculum* for Eve's 'creation', men have had to do without it.[31]

---

30   Personal comment: Mieke Bal.
31   Ziony Zevit, 'The Adam and Eve Story: Eve Came From Where?: Adam and Eve in the Bible', *Bible History Daily* via Biblical Archaelogy, 11 June 2023.

Some rabbis explain that God created man and woman as two separate beings. Others suggest that Adam originally consisted of a male and a female body in one. This first back-to-back creation was not very practical for moving, or having a conversation, so God sawed Adam apart and gave each half a back of their own, before placing the two figures in the Garden of Eden.[32]

An androgynous Adam and Eve sharing two legs, with one arm each. Capital in the church of Anzy-le-Duc, Burgundy. Eleventh century.

The number of artistic creations of Eve grew considerably in ninth-century Europe. In some, the first humans are created separately 'in God's own image'. In others, they are imagined as a combined hermaphrodite creature. The third approach sees God takes a rib from Adam's body and build Eve from that rib.[33]

Halfway through the eleventh century, a crucial reversal took place: Eve's creation was presented in art as an act of Adam's giving birth. She lithely pops out of the sleeping Adam's right

---

32   Ginzberg: *Genesis Rabba in Graves* and Patai: 66; Kvam, Schearing and Ziegler 77–78; Elaine Pagels 1976 p. 298.
33   Englard Yaffa, 'The Creation of Eve in Art and the Myth of Androgynous Adam,' *Ars Judaica* (5) 2009, p. 24.

side, her two hands raised in devotion. An accomplished midwife, God – represented as a man with a beard – pulls Eve from Adam's body with his left hand, while his right hand makes a blessing gesture.

God builds Eve on Adam's giant rib. Miniature from Jacob van Maerlants *Spieghel Historiael*, ca.1325–1335.

Bartolo di Fredi, God as midwife to sleeping Adam and Eve as she gives birth. San Gimignano, fourteenth century.

In Christian Europe the image of a birth-giving Adam was a popular visual theme between the twelfth and the sixteenth century. It can still be seen depicted in churches, cathedrals and museums. A famous example is the scenes of Eve's creation as depicted on the bronze doors of the Baptisterium in Florence, and in Bartolo di Fredi's fourteenth-century fresco in San Gimignano's Collegiata, where creation is presented as procreation with God in the role of midwife.

Representations of Eve born from Adam's body turned the natural roles of men and women upside down, thereby downgrading woman's status as the originator of life. If the one who gives birth is superior to the one who does not, and should rule over the one given birth to, the church had a problem. By underlining that Adam had been Eve's birth-giver, the church resolved the matter of man's superiority over woman.[34] This reversal of roles became written into pedagogic texts, for example, 'A good son loves his father, has respect for him and obeys him, because he has given birth to him, even though his mother provided practical aid.'[35]

Images of Eve appearing from Adam's side or groin as a euphemism for his genitals made clear to the illiterate masses of believers that the man must dominate the wife – he was created first, she came from him and is therefore subservient. This reasoning resulted 'in the natural order of things': that women serve their husbands, children their parents, and servants their lords and masters. This justifies the position of the man as the head

---

34   Augustine (fourth century), one of the most influential Christian church fathers, alleged that 'even before her sin woman had been made to be ruled by her husband and to be submissive and subject to him.' Thus, the inference that Eve's original sin is what marked her as being subservient to man does not carry weight in early Christianity.

35   Italian merchant and writer Paolo da Certaldo (1320–70), *Livre des Bons Usages*, quoted in Zapperi, p. 31.

of the family and his lasting power over his wife and children. The idea that man and woman had been created as equal partners in God's image receded further and further into the background.

The 'crooked rib' in Islamic tradition

The Christian representation of Eve born from Adam went against the biblical creation story and also against its rendition provided in the Quran (Sura 4:1), where no rib is mentioned. Nonetheless, Islamic versions of the rib story spread in Islamic traditions just as freely as in Christian ones.

The character of women became associated with the rib from which Eve was created, according to an Islamic belief that is still quite popular, that a man must learn to live with female 'crookedness'. Women's crooked arguments and unreasonable behaviour are due to the crooked rib she originates from. She cannot help her waywardness and men must try to make the best of it:

> A woman is like a rib; [...]. If you want to straighten her, she will break: if you want to benefit by her, you can do so despite her crookedness.[36]

This text comes from a collection of hadith, the sayings of the Prophet Muhamad. In matters of creation, intelligence and religion, these scriptures present man as superior to woman; therefore, he is more suited to the role of judge and to lead religious services. His testimony is twice as valuable as a woman's.

---

36   Islamic Scholar al-Bukhari (810–70 CE), Arabic-English translation, Vol. VII, Hadith:113: see 'Is the Woman Born of Crooked Rib?' in 'Status and Rights of a Wife in Islam' from *Discourses on Islamic Way of Life* by Mufti Taqi Usmani (db) via Shariah program.

That is why greater responsibilities have been granted him, with accordingly greater privileges.

Various old Islamic texts insist that a man and woman can never be on an equal footing. Often, justification for this reasoning relies on their physical differences. It can be difficult to know how influential these texts are, which are often spread by other groups, such as this text by Ahmad Zaky Tuffaha, used on a Christian missionary website that utilises forged hadith:

> If a woman offered one of her breasts to be cooked and the other to be roasted, she still will fall short of fulfilling her obligations to her husband. And besides that, if she disobeys her husband even for a twinkling of an eye, she would be thrown in the lowest part of Hell, except if she repents and turns back.[37]

Hadith scriptures about the relations between men and women reflect the desperate need for emphasis on the superiority of men. The *Book of One Thousand Questions*, a sort of Islamic catechism in Q&A form, confirms this logic of male superiority on the basis of creation story elements:

Q. Was Adam taken from Lady Eve or was Lady Eve taken from Adam?

A. Lady Eve was taken from Adam. If Adam had been taken from Lady Eve, all men certainly would be obedient to women. So, it is clear that Lady Eve was taken from Adam.

---

37 'Men's Superiority and Women's Deficiency' in *Answering Islam: A Christian-Muslim Dialog* by M. Rafiqul-Haqq and P. Newton.

Q. Was Lady Eve generated from the body of Adam
    or from something outside Adam's body?

A. Lady Eve was generated from the body of Adam.
    If Lady Eve had been generated from something
    outside Adam's body, all women in this world
    certainly would go around naked and not feel
    ashamed in front of men.

Q. Was Lady Eve generated from the left or right side
    of Adam?

A. Lady Eve was generated from the left side of
    Adam. If she had been generated from his right
    side, all women would inherit two parts. Lady Eve
    was generated from the left side of Adam and
    therefore all women only receive one [third] part
    of the inheritance, according to the word of God
    the most high in the Quran.[38]

'The mother of all the living' receives harsh judgement in a
number of commentaries, as the one who disrupted the harmony
of paradise and saddled humanity with the finiteness of life. In
the three monotheistic religions, many theologians were keen on
deploying Eve's sin as an easy means to project negative qualities
on the female sex.

In ancient myths from Mesopotamia, Egypt and Greece,
the Great Mother took care of life and death. In biblical stories,
including those concerning the Garden of Eden, the four rivers,
the Tree of Life and the Serpent, Eve is the cause of the mortality

---

38   Quoted in Steenbrink, *Adam revivus*, 1998 p. 55. Quran Sura 4:1.

of mankind because death did not exist before her disobedience. In the Genesis story, the life-creating role is attributed to God the Father while Eve, the first female creature, brought death into the world – at least in numerous theological comments.[39] So why was it so important to men to monopolise creation myths? Erich Fromm, writing in the twentieth century, summarises that:

> There are good reasons for assuming that even before male supremacy was established there was a 'pregnancy envy' in the male, which even today can be found in numerous cases. In order to defeat the mother, the male must prove that he is not inferior, that he has a gift to produce. Since he cannot produce with a womb, he must produce in another fashion; he produces with his mouth, his word, his thought.[40]

Mysteries surround us. Mankind's way of understanding the world and our place in it is to tell stories that justify the order of things, or the order as we wish it existed. There is no clearer example of this than the journey of creation stories, which morphed from an all-powerful Mother Goddess to a male Supreme Being and subservient female figure. This journey is illustrated not through the deeds or thoughts of man and woman, but through their physical bodies and what they are – or are not – capable of.

---

39 Baring and Cashford: p. 494.
40 Erich Fromm, *The Forgotten Language* (Atlantic Books, 1956) p. 233. More examples of 'pregnancy envy' stories in Chapter 11.

Bumba, creator god of the Kuba-speaking people
in southeastern Congo, throwing up people from
his inner body. Woodcut by South African artist
Motshile wa Nthodi, 1979.

CHAPTER TWO

MALE CREATORS

In the beginning there was only darkness and nothing existed on earth except water. Bumba the Chembe (creator god) ruled alone over this chaos. Bumba had the shape of a man, but was of enormous size [...]. One day he felt a terrible pain in his belly, and soon he began to throw up.[41]

STORIES ABOUT MOTHER EARTH never refer to her longing for her own penis, although she might readily have made that demand. Later goddesses of agriculture were presented with frequent sacrifices of young men, and phalluses were placed on their shrines ready for use.[42]

Creating life with and without a womb

Except in some matrilocal myths, the high-profile creator of life is usually represented as a male divine being. Male gods are also often

---

41 E. Torday and T.A Joyce, *Notes ethnographiques*, (Falk FIls, 1910) pp. 20–21. My translation.
42 Lederer:216.

given anatomical extras in the form of a womb or breasts. Without a womb, Bumba vomits all of creation from his own insides:

> He first vomited the sun, then the moon and lastly the stars, and that is how there came to be light. [...] And Bumba started to vomit again and this time he choked up in sequence the leopard, the crested eagle, the crocodile, a small fish, the tortoise, thunder and lightning, the white heron, the beetle and the goat. He then vomited out a great many people.[43]

Producing the world and humanity, Bumba did as easily without a wife as some birth-giving female creators managed without a husband in earlier traditions. With the exception of thunder and lightning, which soon began to wreak havoc, the Kuba god's life-giving work was flawless.

Hindu goddess Parvati. Tamilnadu, bronze. Eleventh century.

---

43   Torday and Joyce, *ibid. Male Creators.*

Bas-relief Shiva and Parvati. Mount Kailasha, late sixth century.

Similar examples can be found in Hindu mythology, where androgynous gods are a regular occurrence. Shiva and his partner Parvati are often represented in one person: one half is male and the other is female – with the male Shiva usually being the right half.

Prajapati (Lord of Creatures), the creator god of the Vedic period of ancient India, later became associated with the Hindu god Brahma. He brings biological creation into existence and is sometimes seen as the 'motherly male' or referred to as the mythical divinity of birth: 'His structure, his actions, his feelings are all analogous to the human reproductive process; even his lassitude after creation, and his need for refertilisation pertain to this model.' In order to create the world from his insides, he starts with the procreative ritual wish, 'May I propagate myself.'

Then, as the creator, he provides himself with a womb-like organ (*prajanana*), from which he begins to emit 'progeny and animals'.[44]

Androgynous Shiva: right half male, left half female. Khajuraho temple complex, Madhya Pradesh. Tenth century.

Male gods lacking a womb sought different solutions to the problem of procreation. Sometimes Prajapati is represented as a an androgynous divine being in the shape of a man and a woman in an intimate embrace, able to divide itself into two halves in order to copulate:

> Prajapati became pregnant and created posterity from his right thumb, nipple, and other organs, without the benefit of mothers. But he became dissatisfied with this creation, and so he divided his body in half and made one half a woman. He tried to make love to her,

---

44   Doris Meth Srinivasan. *Many Heads, Arms and Eyes* (Brill, 1997) pp. 60–61.

and although she and her brother were shocked at this incestuous act, he eventually married her and created progeny with her.

This raises the tricky question of whether a person originating from your body is your child. If the answer is yes, then having sex with that person is a matter of incest – a universal taboo. From a mythical perspective this problem is done away with as an unavoidable case of 'needs must' in the beginning, there was simply no one else available with whom to multiply and provide an empty world with the first progeny.[45]

What about Adam and Eve? In Christianity the miraculous creation of Eve was sometimes presented as a riddle:

> I died and was not born, I married my father When I
> was one day old,
> And a mother I have none.[46]

The problem of incestuous relations between Adam and Eve was resolved by the influential medieval priest, professor and philosopher Thomas Aquinas who proclaimed that only in the case of a 'natural' birth could one raise the matter of incest, but Eve's was an absolutely exceptional birth. Therefore, Eve was not Adam's daughter.[47]

---

45 Wendy Doniger O'Flaherty, *Women, Androgynes and Other Mythical Beasts* (Chicago University Press, 1980) p. 312.
46 German riddle.
47 Roberto Zapperi, *L'homme enceint*, in L'Homme, Vol 2. 1983:25ff.

Does God have breasts?

The images we came across earlier of goddesses with striking breasts and swollen bellies, found in Europe and up to 40,000 years old, resemble later images from Mesopotamia and Syria's Halaf culture.

Ceramic fertility figurine, Mesopotamia/North Syria. Musée du Louvre, Paris. *c.* 6000–5100 BCE.

Here too believers begged the divine mother to share with them the powers of her mysterious fertility. And here too, since olden times, stories were told in which all life sprang from her fertile motherly body.

Most myths surviving in the Middle East originate from a time in which the exclusive rights of the Mother Goddess had already been transferred to a male partner or a pugnacious rival. That transfer was sometimes far from peaceful. Sometimes the primal foremother was literally butchered by vindictive posterity, as in the famous Babylonian *Enuma Elish* (probably composed in the late second millennium BCE). In this story, the matriarch Tiamat succumbs in a decisive battle with her ambitious offspring Marduk, who then claims power for himself:

> [Marduk] placed his feet on the lower parts of Tiamat
> And with his merciless club smashed her skull.
>   He severed her arteries
> And let the north wind bear up her blood ...

Showing no mercy, he splits her colossal body in two 'like a dried fish' and stands triumphant over her dead remains, which he uses to create the clouds, winds, earth and mountains.[48] His violent settling of accounts renders her powerless.

This cosmic conflict from the Babylonian tradition has been usurped by the biblical myth of a single creator God. However, in poetic biblical texts the actors from older traditions return as sea monsters, dragons and storm gods that are fought against by the Hebrew God. The primal deep, controlled by God's wind sweeping over the 'face of the waters' in the Hebrew Bible is referred to as *tehom*, a term related to Tiamat.[49] The dramatic defeat of the Mother Goddess in Babylonian myth and in the Hebrew Bible is far from unique.[50]

Differing views exist on the development of Judaism – depending on the starting point. In contrast to Marduk, the

---

48   W.G. Lambert in *Imagining Creation*, Geller and Schipper, eds., (Brill, 2008) p. 20.
49   E.g., in Genesis 1:2; 7:11; 8:2; *Oxford Biblical Studies Online*
50   Anne Baring and Jules Cashford. *The Myth of the Goddess. Evolution of an Image*, (Penguin: 1993) 420ff.

Father God has no ancestors. He was there at the beginning, what he said was true, and all he created was good. In the Jewish tradition God had no proper noun, His name was too holy to be uttered aloud, but was reverently referred to as Elohim or El ('God') or as Yahweh (usually translated as 'the Lord') and in expressions such as 'He is One and Only' or as eternal, omnipotent, omnipresent, omniscient, aphysical (and therefore invisible), inscrutable and incomprehensible. Being pure spirit, from the strictly monotheistic perspective of traditional Judaism, He has no body and possesses no sexual traits. Nonetheless, since in the Hebrew language every noun is either masculine or feminine, 'every verbal statement about God conveyed the idea that He was masculine', as Raphael Patai observes in *The Hebrew Goddess*.[51]

> Despite the strict message in the Bible and the Talmud, believers continued to venerate Ashera, Astarte, Anath and other goddesses. Polytheism was current among Israelites until the second century BCE. Patai finds this unsurprising 'in view of the general human, psychologically determined predisposition to believe in and worship goddesses.'[52]

Like earlier representations of Mother Goddesses, Ashera figures from the eighth and seventh century BCE support or offer up their divine breasts with both hands. Referred to in the Canaanite pantheon as 'mother of the gods' and 'wet-nurse of the gods', she was also depicted suckling certain humans of high birth.[53]

---

51   Raphael Patai, *The Hebrew Goddess*, (Wayne State University Press, 1968) 18ff.
52   *Ibid.*; see also The Queen of Heaven WordPress site, accessed 2011 'Does god have breasts?'
53   Patai: 330.

Goddess Ashera. Earthenware, Eretz Israel Museum, Tel Aviv. Eighth to sixth century BCE.

According to archaeologists, Ashera – whose name appears more than forty times in the Bible in a negative context – was the wife of the God of ancient Israel and was worshipped alongside him. Unearthed inscriptions from the eighth century BCE invoke blessings 'by Yahweh and his Asherah'. On an old shard of pottery excavated near Kuntillet Ajrud in the Northern Sinaï, the Egyptian god Bes is the central figure (he looks after sexuality and birth-giving) and beside him is another god (perhaps the militant god Aha). On the same shard, a nameless Jewish merchant has carved: '[...] May you be blessed by the Lord who protects us and his Ashera'.[54]

---

54   Ze'ev Meshel. Kuntillet 'Ajrud. An Israelite Religious Center in Northern Sinai' in *Expedition* 20 (1978): pp. 50–55.

The monotheistic editors who put the Bible into writing twisted the existing stories in a new direction and gave them new meaning. So the Hebrew Bible was bold enough to do what earlier patriarchies hadn't yet dared – to radically obliterate each and every trace of female veneration. The Bible is the first holy book without any female godly presence, divine spouse or lover. In contrast with ancient Middle Eastern deities, Yahweh is the first God unhindered by female competition.[55]

Yahweh is usually characterised by labels such as 'Man of War', 'Hero', 'King', 'Lord of Hosts', 'Master of the Universe' and 'Our Father in Heaven', yet theologians maintain that God is absolutely not to be seen in terms of sex or gender. This was not self-evident to all believers.[56]

The Hebrew Bible emphatically warns against idolatry and the worship of images, which was firmly adopted in Islamic tradition. Christians, on the other hand, frequently represented God visually, mostly in the form of an impressive man with a beard. All three religions refer to God as an anthropomorphic male character, in Judaism and Christianity also called Father – a Father who can get mad at his children:

> The Biblical God-concept [...] reflects the strictly patriarchal order of the society which produced it; this patriarchal society gave rise to a religion centred around a single, universal deity whose will was embodied in the Law, but who was abstract, devoid of all physical

55   Robert Graves and Raphael Patai. *Hebrew Myths: The Book of Genesis* (Anchor Books/Doubleday, 1964) pp. 26–28; 'Bible's Buried Secrets, 2: Did God Have a Wife?' BBC programme; and 'Asherah-Ishtar, Mother Goddess of the Hebrews, wife pf Baal-Yahweh, and Holy Spirit of the Menorah' in Le Mouvement Matricien via WordPress.

56   Elaine Pagels, 'What Became of God the Mother? Conflicting Images of God in Early Christianity' in *Signs* (2) 1976 pp. 293–303.

attributes and yet pronouncedly male, a true projection
of the patriarchal family-head.[57]

As the Jewish tradition developed into a religion with one spiritual
and incorporeal supreme god, believers struggled with this
inexorable requirement. Many still longed for a female element
and found what they needed in local goddesses – which can be
inferred from the many biblical texts in which Hebrew prophets
demonise the worship of goddesses and demand that believers
only worship Him. There are obvious similarities between the
blessings of the breasts and the womb found in Genesis and the
fertility cults of Israelites' Canaanite neighbours, who cherished
goddesses such as Ashera and Anat, represented with prominent
breasts.[58]

In the biblical story in which God makes a covenant with
Abraham, He is referred to as El Shaddai, translated as 'God the
Almighty', but the Hebrew word *shad* means 'breast':

The sacred breast found in early Judaism is directly
connected to God Himself. El Shaddai, the name of
God that is always associated with the fertility blessings,
meant something like the 'God (El) with breasts' or
the 'God who suckles'. Even if this language was to
be understood only metaphorically, it is obviously a
masculine appropriation of a fundamentally female
attribute. God could be seen as both male and female,
transcending the narrow confines of human gender.[59]

---

57 Patai: 23–24.
58 Marilyn Yalom. *A History of the Breast*, (Random House: 1998) 25.
59 Yalom, *ibid.* 27.

By assimilating Ashera's nurturing breasts, the monotheistic God could not only be a Father for his people, but also a comforting Mother and a source of life. The Hebrew Bible refers to God speaking of Himself as a mother 'bearing the Israelites in His bosom'.[60] No less than in the surrounding religions, Judaism celebrated fertility and considered a woman 'complete' once she had given birth to male offspring.[61]

The end of Arab goddesses

As in the Hebrew tradition, the Heaven of the pre-monotheistic Arab world was inhabited by male and female gods. Al-Uzza, Al-Lat and Al-Manat were cherished goddesses in the Arab pantheon of the seventh century. Al-Uzza, the mother of the earth and the equivalent of Demeter, controlled fertility and everything related to the origin of life. Her cult was respected among all the Arabs, 'extended throughout Arabia as far as Mesopotamia [and] enjoyed a privileged importance,' according to Ibn al-Qalbi (737–819) whose *Book of Idols* is one of the most important scriptures about pre-Islamic religions. Evidently, the Prophet Muhammad had to radically shed the surrounding world of Al-Uzza and other Arabian goddesses:

> The cult of the goddesses presented a thorny problem for the messenger of Allah. He would not be able to monopolise power and establish the basis of the monotheistic religion unless these three goddesses were not only discredited but destroyed. Goddesses

---

60   e.g. Isa. 49:1; 49:15; 66:11–13, as mentioned in Walker Bynum, 1982:125.
61   Yalom, *ibid.*; Patai 162.

of fecundity, of generation, of sexual reproduction, they had to be liquidated if Allah and Islam were to triumph. This liquidation was carried out in two ways: ideologically, through discourse; and concretely, through the physical destruction of the sanctuaries of these goddesses.[62]

As in the history of the Hebrews, confusion now spread among the Arabs, who thought the three goddesses were the daughters of Allah (*Banat Allah*). No less than Jewish monotheism many centuries earlier, Islam was confronted with the question of how to get rid of popular goddesses, as Fatima Mernissi explained in *Woman in the Muslim Unconscious*, which she wrote for safety's sake under a pseudonym:

By robbing woman of the giving of life and reducing her to a mere passive envelope in the creation process, God is confronted with the problem of sexual duality: how to retrieve the couple and how to recreate it. It will be reconstituted, but after having undergone a metamorphosis that negates the attribute of femaleness, the capacity to give birth. [...] In sacred reality, it is man who gives birth to woman. [...] For the sacred order to exist, the female element (along with the child as a manifestation of it) has to be liquidated, because it is the incarnation of the finite, the mortal. The pre-Islamic Arab goddesses had to be destroyed to make possible the assertion in heaven and on earth of the domination of the male element – that is, monotheism.'[63]

---

62   Fatna A. Sabbah (Fatima Mernissi), *Woman in the Muslim Unconscious*, 1984 p. 104.
63   *Ibid.* 99, 103.

Al-Uzza's temple in the region east of Mecca was destroyed in 630 CE and sooner or later other sanctuaries suffered a similar fate. Muhammad had to cut the umbilical cord that allied believers with these goddesses. The goddesses do appear in the Quran, but in several passages are deemed a disgrace. According to Ibn al-Qalbi the Quran succeeded in solving the problem[64]; negative stories about Al-Uzza were brought into circulation. An old Berber story contains a warning along those lines:

> Walking through a cemetery at night, you will hear beautiful singing. Whether you want to or not, you will go after it until you find a small, black, but very beautiful girl. She flees from you, first slowly, then more and more rapidly. You are forced to keep up with her and follow her […]. Her breasts grow longer and she ends up by throwing them backwards over her shoulders. Then suddenly she jumps into a grave and the follower, jumping after her, is doomed to jump to his death.[65]

In other words: never go where Al-Uzza and other goddesses are found, because they will mercilessly drag you to your death.

In Judaism, Christianity and Islam, the One, the Eternal, the Almighty, the Supreme God, is mostly presented as male. In Christianity, the Virgin Mary was called upon to fulfil the missing female role and provide a female figure to satisfy the need for 'goddess worship', in particular in its maternal function. Yet despite the persistent messaging centring the male figure in scripture and art in each of the three monotheistic religions, female elements from older mythology and a contemporary

---

64   *Ibid.* 103ff.
65   Ploss and Bartels, *De Vrouw in Natuur – en Volkenkunde Anthropologische Studiën* pp. 128–129. My translation.

desire for woman figures kept sneaking in through unexpected back doors.[66]

Jesus as a woman and a mother

Jesus as a mother is referred to in texts of the earliest Christian church fathers.[67] Around the twelfth century, the image of Jesus with nourishing breasts became very popular in religious scriptures and various sermons refer to Christ nursing his children.

> The Bridegroom [Christ] has breasts, lest he should be lacking any one of all duties and titles of loving kindness. He is the father in virtue of natural creation … And also in virtue of the authority with which he instructs. He is a mother, too, in the mildness of his affection and a nurse.[68]

'Natural creation' suggests here that it is the man who is responsible for procreation (an idea that stubbornly stayed alive for centuries, also outside Christianity), but the metaphor of the nurturing mother perfected that 'natural' image. Of course, the celibate clergy who popularised these motherly depictions had

---

66 As Raphael Patai convincingly demonstrates in *The Hebrew Goddess*. For Jewish gnosticism including female elements, cf. Elaine Pagels, *The Gnostic Gospels*, 1989.

67 Teresa Shaw, *The Burden of the Flesh*, 1998 pp. 16–17; Rolf Quaghebeur, *Eigenzinnige Christusvoorstellingen, over het moederschapsthema in de mystieke beeldtaal van de Middeleeuwen.* With thanks to Elise Bocquet who drew my attention to this unpublished thesis.

68 Caroline Walker Bynum. *Jesus as Mother: Studies in the Spirituality of the High Middle Ages*, 1984 pp. 119, 122. In the Christian Middle Ages there was limited knowledge about the origin of the foetus. Following Aristotle, people believed that the woman contributes the matter for the child and the man provides the superior parts: life and soul.

renounced their own families and were obliged to refrain from all contact with women. Their poetic language served as a spiritual substitute for the world they had relinquished, often at an early age.

The union with God has sometimes been represented as a physical attachment at the nursing breast or within the protective womb. Some monks describe themselves or their souls as brides of Christ. 'One should not exclude that in such texts men could deal with their sexual longing: playing at the breast or penetrating the female body in references (perhaps with womb overtones) to the soul entering the side of Christ.'[69]

A sixteenth-century painting depicts a dead Christ dressed in a loincloth lying on a shroud, surrounded by mourners. His eyes are closed and his knees slightly bent. This Christ has breasts, a fact emphasised by the way his arms are folded, and he holds his right index and middle finger close to the nipple of the left breast, like a woman about to suckle her baby. This gesture has a metaphorical meaning – Jesus' tragic death bestows life on believers and nurtures them, just as a woman gives birth to and nurses her child. Angels, praying women and John the disciple stand around the body, while Mary Magdalene kneels devoutly at Jesus' feet next to her ointment pot. This anonymous painting, entitled *The Lamentation of Christ*, is part of a tradition of representing Christ with breasts.[70] By the end of the fourteenth century, this tradition made way for more emphasis on the suffering of Christ and the sinfulness of man.

---

69   Idem, *Holy Feast and Holy Fast*, 1982 pp. 162–163.
70   The painting is part of the collection of the Musée Hôpital Notre-Dame à la Rose in Lessines, Belgium (with thanks to curator Elise Bocquet who provided the photograph). See also Elaine Pagels, 'What Became of God the Mother? Conflicting Images of God in Early Christianity' in *Signs* (2) 1976 pp. 293–303.

The Lamentation of Christ. Anonymous, sixteenth century.

In the human need for a nursing bosom, androgynous solutions also crop up in other parts of the world. Returning to the birth-giving Indian god Prajapati:

> Prajapati gave himself breasts, so that the creatures he created could suckle and live. Prior, his creatures had famished for want of mother's milk [...]. He then made two breasts teeming with milk in the front of his own body. He (again) emitted offspring. These offspring, having been emitted and rushing to the breasts, thus came into existence; they are those that have not succumbed.[71]

---

71   Doris Meth Srinivasan, *Many Heads, Arms, and Eyes*: pp. 62–63.

The Egyptian god Hapi, who lived in a cave next to the first cataract of the Nile at Elephantine, is another such divine androgynous apparition. His sagging breasts and big belly represented his responsibility for the annual flooding of the Nile and the fertility of its valley.

The androgynous Nile god Hapi, with papyrus and lotus flowers. *Encyclopaedia Biblica*, 1903.

In many cultures male gods adopt characteristics of the other sex,[72] and people have converted their faith in the divine into images that reflect human needs and desires. After Mother

---

72   About Androgyny Worldwide: Hermann Baumann, *Das doppelte Geschlecht*, 1955.

Goddesses were removed or displaced from the religious sphere, crucial female body parts and functions were apparently missed, so patriarchal cultures adroitly projected female features onto male gods and religious figures.

Mary shares her breast milk with the (later canonised) Bernard of Clairvaux.
Grand Curtius Museum, Liège. Flemish School, *c.* 1480.

CHAPTER THREE

GOD THE MOTHER BECOMES THE MOTHER OF GOD

Men and women share equally imperfection, and are to receive the same instruction and the same discipline. For the name 'humanity' is common to both men and women; and for us 'in Christ there is neither male nor female'.[73]

It is not permitted for a woman to speak in the church, nor is it permitted for her to teach, nor to baptise, nor to offer [the eucharist], nor to claim for herself a share in any masculine function – not to mention any priestly office.[74]

IN THE FIRST TWO CENTURIES of Christianity, male and female believers sat together during the service of worship, but it didn't take long before orthodox communities adopted

---

73 Clemens of Alexandria, quoted in Elaine Pagels, *The Gnostic Gospels* (Vintage Books, 1979) p. 87.
74 Tertullian, *ibid.* p. 81.

the traditional Jewish habit of separating men from women. The above quotations represent diametrically opposed views of women by church fathers Clemens of Alexandria and Tertullian from around 180 CE. By the end of the second century, women were forbidden to take charge of any activities in the church. Groups ignoring this prohibition were branded heretics.

Immaculate conception

Both Christians and Muslims consider Mary as holy and elevated above all women. Under her Arabic name Maryam, she is mentioned more often in the Quran than in the Bible. Medieval Islamic scholars saw Maryam as the willing vessel for God's spirit and the Prophet Jesus. She was chosen for her privileged genealogy, carefully preserved chastity and unconditional submission to God.

While the Virgin Mary provided believers with the nourishing maternal breast, time and again the church had to suppress a natural inclination to deify the mother of Jesus: no one was allowed to call her the Mother Goddess.

After some centuries of Christianity, Mary was granted special status. During the ecclesiastical Council of Ephesus in 431 CE she was officially declared to be the 'Mother of God'. It was certainly not by chance that this decision was taken in Ephesus, where the temple of the many-breasted goddess Artemis stood. Early Christianity had been in conflict with this ancient fertility goddess, who had been revered for centuries by Greeks and Asians. In Europe, the Mother of God took the place of the Mother Goddess. The Virgin Mary occupied a special position as a virgin who gave birth to and suckled a divine son. Yet in the Bible only the evangelists Matthew and Luke remark on the virgin birth and even in the book of Luke, Mary calls Joseph the father. Critical Bible specialists consider stories about Jesus's virgin birth more as legends.

Over the centuries, Christian theologians and high clerics elaborated on the metaphor of Mary's virginity. Popes continued to insist that Mary's body was 'intact'. According to Pope Siricius (fourth century CE), Jesus would certainly have rejected Mary as a mother, had she ever been besmirched by male seed. Some clerical scholars asserted that Jesus' delivery had been painless and without afterbirth, and that her hymen remained undamaged.

Even though some theologians, especially Protestant ones, disputed such matters, Roman Catholic and Eastern Orthodox doctrines held on to the virginity of the mother of Jesus.[75]

The oldest images of the Virgin Mary with her child Jesus at the breast originate from the Coptic tradition in Egypt. They were clearly inspired by the example of the goddess Isis affectionately breastfeeding her son Horus.

Egyptian kings were frequently represented at the breast or in the lap of Isis or another goddess, symbolising that they had absorbed the divine powers and status of their powerful nurse.[76] People all over the Mediterranean knew the story of Isis and images of her as a divine nurse have been found throughout Europe. Mary as a human mother with her divine child Jesus appealed to everyone – learned or illiterate, rich or poor – and would have invoked the same feelings of compassion as the Egyptian Mother Goddess. Unsurprisingly, after Christianity had become the most powerful religion in Rome, temples of Isis were forbidden in the city.

---

75   Uta Ranke-Heinemann, *Eunuchs for the Kingdom of God: Women, Sexuality, and the Catholic Church*, 1990 pp. 32 and 34off.

76   More in Baring and Cashford 250; Yalom pp. 11–12.

Isis with her son Horus. Wellcome Collection, London. Bronze, *c.* 600 BCE.

Maria lactans

The nursing Mother of God (referred to in Latin as *Maria lactans* or *Madonna lactans*) inspired many stories and became an important theme in European art. Several famous images depict the miracle of Mary sharing her breast milk with the abbot Bernard of Clairvaux. In paintings and drawings, he kneels down in a white religious habit and the Virgin appears to him while nursing her baby. According to the story, as she takes little Jesus off her breast, a jet of her breast milk curves down to the lips of the clergyman to ease his thirst. In some images the jet of milk lands on his forehead in order to express that this is all about spiritual nourishment.

Some statues of Mary in places of pilgrimage send holy water out through her saintly breasts, so as to generously share the healing forces of the Mother of God with the pilgrims. From a double-sided Maria Fountain in Austria, the curing water wells from four breasts at the same time.

There have been many stories of sightings of the Holy Virgin over the centuries. They have all been mapped by *National Geographic*, both those approved and not approved by the Vatican.[77] In Europe, Mary's multiple apparitions of 1858 at Lourdes are well known, but more than three centuries earlier, in 1531, she appeared in Mexico City on four occasions to Juan Diego, a poor Indian who was belatedly canonised in 2002. A basilica dedicated to the Virgin of Guadalupe (as the Mother of God is called there), near the site of the apparitions, is visited every year by twenty million pilgrims.

The religious becomes secular

Symbols can make an invisible reality accessible but once they hit their peak, they gradually lose their power and ultimately, their meaning. This is what happened, slowly but surely, to the symbol of Mary's bared breast. Although representations of the maternal breast had been consistently portrayed, unnoticed changes tainted its symbolic structure, as Margaret Miles explains in *A Complex Delight* (2008). Studying hundreds of images of Mary suckling her child, she noticed a shifting meaning and function of women's breasts in early modern Western Europe – a meaning visibly evolving from the religious to the secular:

---

[77] '500 Years of Virgin Mary Sightings in One Map', *National Geographic*, 13 November 2015.

In early modern Western societies in which Christianity was the dominant religion, her bared breast, appearing in paintings and sculptures, signified nourishment and loving care – God's provision for the Christian, ever in need of God's grace. Moreover, referencing every human being's earliest pleasure, the breast pointed to and 'opened up' the greater reality of the universe's provision and sustenance of life. The believer's acceptance, pleasure and gratitude, expressed by the appropriate responses, reminded viewers of the foundational moment of their existence.[78]

Two statues of the Virgin breastfeeding Jesus.
Left: Lorraine, France, Musée des Arts Décoratifs, Paris, early fifteenth century.
Right: Lower Austria, German National Museum, Nuremberg, c. 1380.

---

78   Miles, 2008 p. ix.

Virgin Mary feeding her child, surrounded by angels. Crete, second half of the fifteenth century.

From the fourteenth to the eighteenth century, Mary was frequently depicted with one bared breast suckling Christ as an infant. The image aligned with the natural act of mothers everywhere, whether at home or in the public sphere, exposing a breast to feed their baby without embarrassment. Thanks to Mary's indispensable nursing breast, Jesus could later give his life to save the world. Thus, in a certain sense, the Virgin Mary's milk was equated with the blood of Jesus.[79] The Mother of God was often seen as a mediator: she pleaded with her divine son for the sake of mortals who were terrified of the Last Judgement. In some stories her breasts even alleviated the concerns of those who had already died. In an Italian painting by Nicola Filotesio dell'Amatrice (1506), Mary with Jesus on her right arm stands high above Purgatory, where she lets the milk from her breasts rain down upon the thirsty souls.

---

79   Saxon, Elizabeth, *The Eucharist in Romanesque France: Iconography and Theology*, 2006 pp. 205–207.

In early images, a breast about the size of a billiard ball pops up from a small aperture in Mary's royal raiment, often placed awkwardly high on her shoulder. And until well into the fifteenth century believers associated Mary's one bared breast with her virginal motherhood:

> No more bare flesh than was absolutely necessary surrounded this single nourishing breast – it was solemn and not sensuous, and the clothing worn by the Virgin in all early fifteenth century art was equally solemn. These gowns were similar to a type of dress actually in use, but they were much enriched and manipulated for hieratic purposes in art.[80]

By 1750 the symbolic meaning of the nursing mother's breast was no longer understood, thanks to increasing eroticisation and medicalisation of this body part.

From as early as the fourteenth century, people had started to adapt their bodies by all manner of artificial means: both men and women embellished their contours with shape-improving ribs and paddings. Corsets became fashionable and breasts were constricted or pushed up.[81]

Buttoned up

Little by little, three changes took place in paintings of breasts, as Margaret Miles discusses in great detail in *A Complex Delight*. First, the breast was depicted more and more realistically and

---

80   Anne Hollander, *Seeing Through Clothes* (University of California Press, 1978) p. 187.
81   As shown in the exhibition La Mécanique des Dessous in the Musée des Arts Décoratifs, Paris, 2013.

the increased emotional and erotic implications provoked clerical fear of arousal. Male priests in Catholic regions became aware that the increasingly lifelike images no longer produced the same unequivocal meaning. No wonder then that in December 1563 the Council of Trento rejected realistic images of the nursing Holy Virgin as unseemly.

From the end of the fifteenth century, biblical maternal breasts were not the only breasts to be painted or sculpted. Aside from the Virgin Mary, breasts played a role in other biblical topics – such as representations of the story of the elders peeping upon the bathing Susanna – and in tragic classical themes such as Lucretia committing suicide after being a victim of rape. A seventeenth-century example is *The Prodigal Son* by Johannes Baeck, a painting expressing the moral degradation of a young man whose hand is carelessly groping the naked breast of a woman.

The Prodigal Son by Johannes Baeck, Kunsthistorisches Museum, Vienna, 1637.

Other paintings on a biblical theme depict the wife of Potiphar trying to seduce the innocent slave Joseph with her breasts. The moral lesson of chastity was given less and less emphasis:

> By the seventeenth century, naked breasts presented frankly erotic images, though often still with scriptural warrant […]. In the eighteenth century, unapologetically secular breasts, larger and rounder than a century before, were frequently painted.[82]

A third change to be seen in early modern art was that not only one but two breasts were depicted, whether or not framed in a *décolleté*. A transitory figure in this development was Mary Magdalene. As a former sex worker, good and evil come together in her sexualised body, 'migrating between the repentant sinner and the erotic sex worker'. A Donatello statue hides her breasts chastely behind her long hair, but in Titian's painting the nipples are clearly visible through her long hair.[83]

In the second half of the fifteenth century *décolletage* became fashionable in Europe thanks to Agnès Sorel, a renowned beauty of her time who became famous as the mistress of Charles VII of France. In the mid fifteenth century this celebrity courtesan modelled for Jean Fouquet's *La Vierge de Melun*. He painted her with her eyes piously lowered, crowned and surrounded by angels, with a naked baby Jesus sitting upright beside her and one uncovered breast directly in view. In an anonymous later painting she is wearing a long black dress and a gauze veil, repeating the same pious downward glance. From her loosely laced bustier one naked breast emerges, even though there is no child on her

82   Miles: pp. 8–9.
83   Miles: pp. 11–13.

lap. Instead she holds a book in her hand with a finger halfway between the pages, suggesting that she was reading while waiting for the painter.

Left: *La Vierge de Melun* by Jean Fouquet, Royal Museum of Fine Arts, Antwerp, *c.* 1450. Right: Portrait of Agnès Sorel. Anonymous, after Fouquet. Château de Loches, Indre-et-Loire, sixteenth-century.

No doubt this painting shocked spectators at the time, as it went against the unwritten rule that the artist must convey religious meaning to believers:

> [...] contrary to pictorial custom, [Agnès Sorel] wears a very low décolletage and fashionable tight bodice, ostentatiously unlaced to liberate a most attractive large white breast. This breast bursts out of its confinement while the other one, for once equally

visible under the dress, submits to its pressure with equally sexy effect.[84]

Such paintings reflected the transition from religious images with no implicit aesthetic purpose to 'art for art's sake'.

Sorel introduced her daring fashion of keeping her bodice unlaced to expose her naked breasts at the French court shortly before her untimely death at twenty-eight in 1450. Many women followed her habit, as can be seen in other European paintings. Piero di Cosimo's portrait of Simonetta Vespucci as Cleopatra is a famous example.

Piero di Cosimo, portrait of Simonetta Vespucci as Cleopatra. Genoa, 1490.

84   Anne Hollander, 1978 pp. 187–188.

The long-cherished symbolism of Mary's bare maternal breast gave rise to opposing views: either degraded as an object of lust or rejected on the grounds of chastity. From now on, the owners of flesh-and-blood breasts could be dismissed as wicked seducers or eulogised as pious, chaste madonnas. Breasts became a social standard by which to judge women's chastity, or lack of it.

These views quickly escalated. Within a century of the invention of printing in around 1440, Europe was inundated with illustrated pornographic literature.[85] By the seventeenth century, images of the female body were circulating in numerous medical textbooks, such as Vesalius' famous book on human anatomy, with its title page showing a female body being dissected before a mass of male spectators. Through the twin rise of pornography and medical research, those body parts that only ornament the female body became special objects of attention in new spheres.

But what of Mary? As the Mother of God she had been the indispensable link between God the Father and ordinary men and women. Local colour was projected onto her everywhere. In Europe artists gave her white, Western features: blue eyes, rosy cheeks and even fair hair. On other continents her skin colour, eye shape, facial features and dress matched those of local believers, so that people could more easily identify with her. In Africa and Latin America, she became darker skinned. In China she resembled Guanyin, the kind and compassionate goddess of mercy, while in Vietnam she became popular as 'Our Lady of La Vang', wearing the *ao dai* national dress. It was in La Vang in 1798 that Mary appeared in that outfit to believers who had fled to the jungle, at a time when the Vietnamese emperor was persecuting and killing Christian believers.

---

85   cf. Miles p. 132: 'A search of *Art Resource* in New York, the largest image collection in North America, produced not a single image of the virgin with one bare breast after 1750.

Title page of Andreas Vesalius' *De humani corporis fabrica*, Basel. Leiden University Libraries, 1543.

Image of the black Virgin Mary on the island of Gorée off the coast from Senegal.

Over time, European Catholic missionaries distributed millions of devotional pictures of Mary all over the world. They all have one striking feature in common: the Mother of God no longer suckles the baby Jesus, but wears buttoned-up dresses in accordance with the decree of the Council of Trento, thereby effectively obliterating the previously familiar and well-understood image of the Blessed Virgin as a nursing mother.

PART II

DESIRABLE AND TERRIFYING

Above: Fertility ornaments, vulva with womb. Flores, Indonesia.
Below left: Necklace pendant, silver with cedar wood, Tuareg, Sahara; right: Necklace pendant, leather triangle with fertility cowrie shell, Dogon, Mali. Author's collection, twentieth century.

CHAPTER FOUR

THE GATEWAY OF LIFE

The nameless is the beginning of Heaven and Earth.
The named is the mother of ten thousand things.
Ever desireless, one can see the mystery. Ever
desiring, one can see the manifestations. [...]
Darkness within darkness.
The gate to all mystery.[86]

Mother of the feast, little stone in your vulva.
Oo! Oo! The vertical column of the clitoris, vulva.
Oo-ee-ee!
Penis. O! Penis. O! Vagina is calling you.[87]

Dutch columnist Frits Abrahams rightly marvelled at the negative
language referring to the female sex apparatus in his part of the
world. In Dutch, an off day is called a 'cunt day': 'Cunt is nothing,
cunt is feckless, cunt is something extremely bad.'[88] He noticed
that women use the word for their own body part as derogatively

---

86   *Tao Te Ching*, translated by Gia-fu Feng and Jane English (1972), Chapter 1.
87   E.E. Evans-Pritchard, *Some Collective Expressions of Obscenity in Africa*, 1929 p. 323.
88   NRC newspaper, back page.

and as indifferently as men. Moreover, in his recollection, the absolute lowest term 'supercunt' was used by women only.[89]

The time has come to speak up for this unjustly reviled body part, the pathway to life for all humanity. This chapter explores the vulva and removes some of the veils that usually obscure it.

The 'Mystery'

My grandmother never spoke about female genitalia except once when, with great hesitation, she referred to the vagina as 'The Mystery'. She was part of a long tradition where this 'gateway of life' was not referred to directly, on account of its possession of unknown powers.

In different parts of the world women were believed to be able to protect their family or the whole community against impending disaster thanks to this hidden mystery. Even an amulet with an image of the vulva could put enemies to flight and protect against evil. This belief comes from a much older belief that if one or several women dare to expose their awesome genitals to a rainless sky, infertile fields, turbulent seas or dangerous enemies, predators will flee, natural disasters will be calmed and people's fertility and good harvests will be secured.

This custom may appear vulgar to contemporary onlookers, but the word 'obscene' includes the meaning 'inauspicious'. In times of danger, during the historical transition from hunting to agriculture, many peoples practised this rite. Deliberately and solemnly exposing one's genitals was considered an act of exceptional courage and only applied in extreme situations: 'In normal times the abnormal is taboo, but in abnormal times

---

89   'Van kut naar superkut', NRC *Handelsblad*, 27 February 2017.

abnormal things are done to restore the normal condition of affairs.'[90]

In ancient China, in times of serious drought female priests were ritually undressed and exhibited to the heat of the sun to call down rain. Indeed, magic power was attributed to the naked female body:

> As the ultimate embodying of yin, people attributed to the publicly-shown female genitals the power to eliminate all yang. In emergency cases Chinese generals sometimes resorted to naked prostitutes to silence the cannons of their adversaries.[91]

Deterrence of the enemy by the display of genitals was also practised in other parts of the world. By revealing their vulva in public in dramatic circumstances, women could guarantee the wellbeing of their own clan. In times of war, the effect was twofold: the soldiers on one's own side were encouraged and opponents were paralysed by this deadly threat.

Such exposure, as documented by Edward Schafer in his paper, 'Ritual Exposure in Ancient China', was a rare event, imbued with magical power. The shaman's exposed yin counteracts the yang of the burning sun or, in another explanation, the nudity shames the rain-dragons into action.

In the Niger Delta in July 2002, a group of six hundred unarmed mothers and grandmothers drew on this ancient curse during an oil protest by threatening to remove all their clothes –

90   E.E. Evans-Pritchard, 'Some Collective Expressions of Obscenity in Africa', in *The Journal of the Royal Anthropological Institute of Great Britain and Ireland*, 1929 p. 323.

91   Wilt Idema, 'Bespied in bad', p. 31 in De Boekenwereld 2017; Edward H. Schafer, 'Ritual Exposure in Ancient China', in *Harvard Journal of Asiatic Studies* Vol. 14, No. 1/2 (1951) pp. 130–184.

and it worked. In the context of the ancestral tradition that 'we all come into the world through the vagina', the wordless gesture of exposing the vulva includes a powerful message:

> 'Herewith we take back the life we have given you.' The curse publicly punishes men with social execution and considers them to be dead: as from now all women would refuse to cook for them, marry them or do business with them. Here, as in earlier days, the 'Curse of Nakedness' proved to be a most effective female weapon to ward off misery and disaster.[92]

Sheela-na-gig at the church of Kilpeck, Herefordshire, twelfth century.

---

92   More information in *Naked or Covered*, pp. 28–29.

Dilukái, Palau, The Michael Rockefeller Memorial Collection, *c.* 1900.

In northern Europe there are many examples of old stone carvings of female figures with gaping vulvas. In Great Britain and Ireland they are called *sheela-na-gig*. These images were believed to avert death or evil spirits. In the Pacific Island country of Palau, carved wooden female figures were fixed over the doorway of a chief's house: the figures' hands rest on their thighs and their splayed legs reveal a striking vulva and clitoris marked by a dark triangle. As elsewhere, such images, called *Dilukái*, were meant to protect health and fertility, guarantee a good harvest and fend off evil spirits. Each of these iterations represent the vulva as 'the primordial gate, the mysterious divide between non-life and life.'[93]

---

93   Juliette Dor, 'The Sheela-na-Gig: An Incongruous Sign of Sexual Purity' in Bernau, Evans and Salih, 2003 pp. 33–55; Bertling 96ff; Mircea Eliade in the *Encyclopedia of Religion*.

From the breasts of the respectfully invoked Yoruba Mother Goddess Jemaya spring all streams fertilising the land, but male fascination with divine nourishing breasts invariably comes with mixed feelings. She deserves respect, but the divine mother remains a fickle creature to be approached with care. An old Yoruba song full of underlying anxieties refers to the powers of 'the Mothers', a collective term acknowledging the special powers of women, elderly, ancestral or deified:

> Honour, honour today, oooooo.
> Honour to my mother […]
> Mother whose vagina causes fear to all. Mother whose pubic hair bundles up in knots. Mother who sets a trap, sets a trap …[94]

The primal gateway as a curse (and its resolution) in times of crisis is alive and well in the Yoruba tradition.

Dark threat

Mythological stories present scenes in which a 'goddess of obscenity' unveils her intimate body parts in a ritual dance at times of crisis, evoking the sacred cycle of fertility, life and death. In ancient Japanese myth, Susanoo, brother of the sun goddess Amaterasu, is a disruptive element in the realm of the gods. His rage makes the lush green landscape wither, threatening human life. His parents, the creator gods Izanagi and Izanami, decide to ban their uncouth son to the underworld of Yomi. Before

---

94   A.B. Ellis, *The Yoruba-speaking Peoples*, 1894 pp.43–44; Drewal in African Arts 7 (2), 1974 p. 60.

his departure Susanoo is granted one last visit with Amaterasu in the Plain of High Heaven. As soon as he ascends, he causes violent commotion in the sea and deafening groans in the hills and mountains. He then desecrates the sacred Weaving Hall, where the garments of the gods are woven, and the consequences are disastrous. The raging Sun Goddess gathers her radiant robes about her, enters a cave, obstructs the entrance with a rock and hides in seclusion. Suffocating darkness swallows every trace of daylight: a fatal catastrophe threatening all life.

As the gods ponder how to persuade Amaterasu to show herself again in all her lustrous glory, the heavenly maze goddess steps forward. Dancing in a trance, she first takes out her breasts and then lowers her robe below the vulva. The gathered gods roar with liberating laughter, awakening Amaterasu's curiosity. As she eases the cave door ajar and her divine light comes forth again, the god of force Tajikarao takes her hand and pulls her out into the open. All the gods align behind her so she can't go back inside. As the sun's light shines again in Heaven as on Earth, Susanoo is punished and the end of humanity has been averted.[95]

In Greek mythology the goddess of agriculture Demeter curses the fertile earth after her beloved daughter Persephone is kidnapped by the god of the underworld. Because of that curse no more children are born, corn refuses to grow, flowers stop blooming and people lose their faith in the gods. After gloomy wanderings over the earth, Demeter sinks down near a well, where Baubo crosses her path. This mysterious figure succeeds in making

---

95   F. Hadland Davis. *Myths and Legends of Japan*, 1912. This story originates from the Kojiki, or *Records of Ancient Matters* (translated from the Japanese by Basil Hall Chamberlain in 1882). At the order of Empress Gemmyo, this old and very long oral story was performed in 712 CE by an old woman narrator who knew it by heart. It was then transcribed for the first time – cf. Nobuhiro Matsumoto. *Essai sur la Mythologie Japonaise*, 1928 and Pierre Lévêque, *Colère, Sexe, Rire: Le Japon des Mythes Anciens*, 1988.

the goddess smile again. Is she another deity, an old midwife, or perhaps Demeter's former nurse? There are different opinions. Her name means 'lap' or 'belly' and she personifies sexuality – images show her with a vulva on her chin or conspicuously visible between her spread legs. She gestures to her naked genitals and puts her hand there. To please Demeter, Baubo has shaved her pubic area and begins to dance with swinging breasts and wiggling hips, suggesting the act of sex. As the goddess of agriculture, Demeter's deep sadness – that becomes explosive anger – is a terrible threat to humanity's future. As in the Japanese story, unveiling the vulva undoes the spell in this Greek myth.[96]

Demeter on her throne, with ears of corn, poppies and a torch. Corinthian earthenware, National Archaeological Museum, Athens, late fifth century BCE.

During the festivities in honour of Demeter, which were widely practised in ancient Greece, only women could access the central secret ceremony. The cakes eaten there were in the shape of genitals and women amused each other by telling obscene jokes during a

---

96   Images of Baubo have been found in many places, mainly in Greek settings. With thanks to Leiden University colleagues Ineke Sluiter and John Miguel Versluys for personal information about Baubo.

meal accompanied with abundant wine. The Baubo ceremony of Anasyrma – the exposing of the genitals – concluded the fertility rites.[97]

In agrarian contexts, obscenity served to 'reanimate' fertility. The gesture of exposure was unprecedentedly powerful and interpreted as a favourable portent. Thanks to their birth-giving gateway, women had the power to dispel imminent catastrophe, to melt away anger in contagious laughter and to create space for new vigour and a future full of new life.

Mounds of terracotta, gold or lapis lazuli

As long as the Great Goddess was in high esteem, holy rivers welled up from the vagina of the earth and all life crept out of her birth canals onto the earth. The best-known symbol for the vulva is the inverted triangle, the Greek letter Δ (delta). Uninverted, the same symbol refers to a river mouth. In ancient Greece, Delta was a place of sanctuary for Demeter, originally worshipped as Mother Goddess and later held responsible for agriculture.

The inverted triangle indicates ancient foremother or goddess images in many cultures. Corresponding to the *Dilukái* figure from Palau, an image of the Sumerian goddess Ishtar on a water pot uses the triangle to symbolise the vulva and the womb. Ishtar was the Sumerian goddess of love and war. In ancient Mesopotamia her vulva was admired and praised as 'sweet as beer' and 'sweet as the mouth'.[98]

97 P–L. Couchoud, 'Le mythe de la danseuse obscène' in *Mercure de France*, July–August 1929. Paris.

98 With thanks to Assyriologist Theo Krispijn, Leiden University, for information and references to the *Reallexicon der Assyriologie*.

Ishtar among water animals, representing fertility. Larsa, Mesopotamia, Musée du Louvre, Paris. Second millennium BCE.

Earthenware 'casserole' with marked vulva and double row fertility triangles as border decoration. Death gift, Syros, 2800–2300.

Aside from the triangle, the vulva is represented as a lozenge or diamond in many cultures. A gold, triangular-shaped pendant from the third millennium BCE unearthed in Syria includes an inserted lozenge of twisted gold wire that represents the vulva. Before the civil war, this fertility ornament was on show in the

Museum of Aleppo.[99] The Renault logo is another such stylised diamond, though it is doubtful that many car drivers are aware of the symbol's profound meaning or protective qualities.

Renault logo

In moments of existential crisis, threat or illness in the ancient world, votive offerings or oblations would be left on a shrine to appease a god or goddess, confirm an entreaty or express thanks for a wish fulfilled. In many cultures, these ornaments were in the form of female genitals. On the opening page of this chapter are two examples from the island of Flores in Indonesia. In ancient times warriors wore these amulets as a means of protection when they went to war. Two more originate from Africa – one logenze-shaped and one incorporating the natural contours of a cowrie shell. Vulva-shaped objects dedicated to the goddess were sometimes made of expensive materials. One gold vulva and eight silver vulvas feature on a millennia-old clay tablet list of votives dedicated to the goddess Ishtar. One of the associated prayers runs as follows:

---

99   Cf. Rients de Boer, *De kleding van Ištar van Lagaba*, 2013:30ff.

Merciful Ishtar, who reigns over the universe,
Heroic Ishtar, who creates humanity,
You who walk on ahead of the flock, you who love the
     shepherd [...]
Without you the river will not open,
The life-giving river will not be blocked up,
Without you the channel will not open,
The channel from which people drink far and wide
Will not be closed [...]
Ishtar, charitable lady,
Hear me and bestow your grace upon me.

At the end of this prayer Ishtar is discreetly reminded of all the sacrifices the humble servant has brought her; a comprehensive inventory ending with the most expensive gifts: 'a vulva of lapis lazuli and a [missing word] of gold.'[100] Vulva- or womb-shaped votives made of stone, terracotta and other materials exist in many traditions. For an ancient Roman votive example, see the opening page of this chapter.

As well as being an ancient fertility symbol, the vulva has always been thoroughly discussed in manuals devoted to eroticism and sex. The Indian *Kama Sutra* dates to the second century and served as a walk-through for men and women in whose arranged marriages love did not usually spontaneously bloom. Sex manuals also circulated early in China.[101] In Arabic there is *The Perfumed Garden of Sensual Delight*, the long treatise written by Sheikh al-Nefzawi, each edition of which looked different. Such books give an idea of the kind of women the various authors consider 'worthy

---

100 Erich Ebeling, *Quellen zur Kenntnis der Babylonischen Religion*, Leipzig, 1918, II:12. My translation.

101 Robert van Gulik's *Sexual Life in Ancient China* (1961) is an erudite and detailed book on this topic.

of praise' or 'deserving nothing but contempt', as al-Nefzawi put it.[102] This is how he saw the ideal woman:

> In order that a woman may be relished by men, she must have a perfect waist, and must be plump and lusty. [...] her breath will be of pleasant odour, her throat long, her neck strong, her bust and her belly large; her breasts must be full and firm; her belly in good proportion, and her navel well-developed and marked; the lower part of the belly is to be large, the vulva projecting and fleshy from the point where the hairs grow to the buttocks; the conduit must be narrow and not moist, soft to the touch, and emitting a strong heat [...]. If one looks at a woman with those qualities in front, one is fascinated; if from behind, one dies with pleasure.[103]

And so forth. Finally, a brief quotation from a Chinese manual (Ming Dynasty, 1368–1644) in which the author discerns different kinds of vulvas:

> All vulvas, whether in the high, middle, or low positions, possess desirable qualities, provided that someone knows how to use them well. A woman whose vulva is in the middle [...] is suitable for copulation in all four seasons of the year and for induction into all sexual positions. [...] A woman whose vulva is high is suitable

---

102   *The Perfumed Garden of Sensual Delight* (الروض العاطر في نزهة الخاطر) is an Islamic sex manual, similar to the Hindu *Kama Sutra*. It is believed to have been written between 1410 and 1434 CE. Published in Paris in a first full French edition in 1886 as *Le Jardin Parfumée du Cheikh Nefzaoui: Manuel d'Erotologie Arabe: xvi Siècle*, Sir Richard Burton took care of an English translation from the French in the same year.

103   Sheikh Nefzawi, *The Perfumed Garden* (Panther Books, 1886) p. 96.

for cold winter nights. A man can have intercourse with
her by lying on her under the coloured quilts of a square
bed. A woman whose vulva is low and placed further
towards the back is suitable especially for hot summers.
A man can have intercourse with her by sitting on a
stone bench under the shade of bamboo. [...] This is
what is called utilising the particular advantages of the
shape of the woman one copulates with.[104]

Utagawa Hiroshige, Spring Night, Honolulu Museum of Art, CJGC.
The right-hand page reads: 'One hour of spring night (= sex) is billions worth yen.'

---

104   Quoted in R.H. van Gulik, *Sexual Life in Ancient China: A Preliminary Survey of Chinese Sex and Society* from *c.* 1500 BCE till 1644 CE, 1974 pp. 272–273.

Gnashing teeth and other terrors

The Ill-Matched Couple, copper engraving by Hans Baldung Grien. State Art Collections of Dresden, 1507.

In contexts where an exposed vulva is believed to eliminate negative forces or drive away hostile armies, it is understandable that individual fears of the vulva give rise to fantasies about fearsome vaginas. Insatiable female lust is part of that fear. A man needs boldness and self-confidence. Uncertainty about whether one's potency can match one's partner's appetite, especially for older men, is a delicate point: 'Old man, cold bedfellow' as the saying goes.

It is the old man's nightmare that his young wife runs off with a younger, more adequate sexual partner. As far as ageing is concerned, Bette Midler's wisdom in her twentieth-century TV show applies to all times and places: 'It is easier for a man of twenty with a woman of eighty than the other way round.' But impotency is not always put down to a matter of age.

Anthropologists working around the world have described a number of incidents where men have believed that male impotence has been deliberately caused by women's special powers. Among the Australian Aranda, it was feared that a woman might have scattered a handful of bewitched dust on the place where the man usually went to pee, which would give him a burning feeling in his urethra and unbearable pain. Or that if she sings a magic song over her own forefinger and then inserts it in her vulva, the man who has sex with her will 'become diseased and may lose his organ altogether'.[105]

In New Zealand, the Maori tradition warns against the vagina as 'the house of death'. Male fear in some cases changes women into inhuman creatures, as in this Khond story from India: 'In the old days, woman had four breasts and two vaginas, one in front and one behind. But she had only one face, looking forwards. Most *people* were so frightened of *women* that they never got married'[106]. In stories from Asia and America, the first created women used to consume their food with vaginal teeth. *Vagina dentata* stories in which women eat or rob men's most vulnerable body part reflect male nightmares. One such myth depicts a Jicarilla Apache demon daughter, with a toothed vagina. The demon changes herself into a beautiful girl as soon as she sees a man, seduces him, bites off his penis and eats it. The vulnerable penis is then confronted by all sorts of extreme threats: elephant tusks, poisonous snake teeth, a saw at the entrance of the vagina, and hungry piranhas waiting within. The horror, the horror![107]

In some stories the woman herself doesn't seem to realise how dangerous she is, even though the man hears the gnashing teeth

---

105   Ernest Crawley, *The Mystic Rose: A Study of Primitive Marriage*, 1902:182ff.
106   Elwin 1954 p. 452.
107   Yukaghir story from Siberia, other examples and details: *In the Beginning There Was No One*, Chapter 8.

under her skirt from afar. Of course, a real hero does not give up, but employs smart tactics. Before knocking at her dangerous gate, he may lovingly rock the woman to sleep, courageously remove those horrifying teeth by pulling them with a cord or destroying them with an iron rod and, to his great relief, discover a 'normal' vagina beneath. As soon as the woman (read: vagina) has been tamed, the threat disappears once and for all.[108]

Sometimes the woman is completely innocent: in a Gond story from Central India, a small snake slips inside the vagina of someone squatting down to relieve herself. There the intruder grows so rapidly that her husband thinks she's pregnant, but one day, in full public view at a bazaar, the head of the snake pops out from under her sari. A passer-by who sees it immediately realises how much danger her husband is in (in the story, no one seems to care much that the woman too might be in peril). The snake is killed and from then on, the couple live happily ever after.[109]

Origin stories about sex reveal fear of 'the first time'. A Chilean Mapuche proverb classifies women as sexually violent: 'They overthrow even a man's penis.' The widespread idea that female powers must be 'tamed' by men through sex fits with earlier lines of thought about the need for the power of the Great Goddess to be usurped by an almighty male creator god. 'The penis comes erect as if it intends to kill, but the vagina swallows and tames it,' is a concise Nigerian Igbo observation.

Man knows he must take the initiative during sex, because women taking the lead is suspect or taboo. Stories in which the first, still untamed woman dares to take the initiative or wants to lie on top, concern themselves with the need to radically

---

108 Bogoras, Waldemar. *Chukchee Mythology*, 1913 p. 667; Ho Ting-jui, *A Comparative Study of Myths and Legends from Formosan Aborigines*. Unpublished thesis, Indiana University, 1967 p. 388.

109 Elwin, 'The Vagina Dentata Legend' in *British Journal of Medical Psychology* 19 p. 443.

eliminate threatening female power. The Jewish Talmud tells the story of Lilith, Adam's first wife, who demanded the impossible:

> Adam said, 'I will not lie beneath you, but only on top.
>   For you are fit only to be in the bottom position,
>   while I am to be in the superior one.'
> Lilith responded, 'We are equal to each other
>   inasmuch as we were both created from earth.'[110]

Following that line of argument, Lilith insisted on lying next to him, or on top. When Adam tried to force her into his preferred position, she refused to give in, sneered at him and flew away, out of paradise. Lilith went to the shores of the Red Sea where she cohabited with lascivious demons. Her favourite pastime was having sex with them. Angels wanted to bring Lilith back to Adam, but she refused and became a demon herself, giving birth to a hundred evil demons daily. To this day Lilith and her daughters, the *lilim*, kill babies, preferably uncircumcised little boys. Taking inspiration from their mother, the *lilim* hang around in men's dreams, sit on their victims' bodies, and gulp down the poor men's semen as they ejaculate. With the stolen semen, they continue to produce yet more new demon children. Though there are many different versions of this story, the storytellers all agree that Lilith, Adam's assertive wife, wanted complete equality, even in matters of sex. God took pity on Adam, let him fall into a deep sleep and created Eve, 'flesh of his flesh' (Genesis 2:23).

Monotheistic theologians were inclined to rule over the

---

110   The *Alphabet of Ben Sira* 5:23 a and b. This is the oldest source of the Lilith story (eighth to tenth century). For more references see Kvam, Schearing aand Ziegler 1999 p. 204. An earlier reference to Lilith as Lilake has been found on a Sumerian clay tablet of 2000 BCE, cf. Graves and Patai p. 68. The only reference to Lilith in the Bible is in the book of Isaiah (34:14).

uncontrollable reality of the female body. According to Christian theologian Rosemary Radford Ruether in her book *Sexism and God-Talk*, 'even in the original, unfallen creation, woman would have been subordinate and under the dominion of man ... the woman should have deferred to the man, who represents, in greater fullness than herself, the principle of "headship" mind or reason. He, in turn should regard her as representing the part of himself that must be repressed and kept under control by reason to prevent a fall into sin and disorder.' Church Father Augustine (fourth century) observed that 'even before her sin [Eve] had been made to be ruled by her husband and to be submissive and subject to him.' After the loss of paradise, 'woman's suppression must be redoubled. Proneness to sin and disorder is no longer potential but actual, and woman is particularly responsible for it.'[III]

Similarly Islamic orthodox theology recommends a wife's obedience to her husband as the key to Paradise. Both Al-Bukhari and Imam Muslim report:

Abu Hurairah (May Allah be pleased with him) reported:

Messenger of Allah (ﷺ) said, "When a man calls his wife to his bed, and she does not respond and he (the husband) spends the night angry with her, the angels curse her until morning".

Messenger of Allah (peace and blessing be upon him) said, "By Him in Whose Hand is my life, when a man calls his wife to his bed, and she does not respond,

---

III   Ruether, Rosemary, *Sexism and God-Talk: Toward a Feminist Theology* (Beacon Press, 1993)

the One Who is above the heaven becomes displeased with her until he (her husband) becomes pleased with her."[112]

A little stone in the vulva

Does a man enjoy sex more than a woman, or the other way around? Even the gods once wondered. The Roman god Jupiter believed that women enjoyed it more than men, but his wife Juno disagreed. They submitted their question to Tiresias, a wise soothsayer and prophet in Thebes who had lived in a female body for seven years. Tiresias, who had been born a man, became a woman after he struck two copulating snakes with a stick. Seven years later he saw the same snakes copulating again and a second blow with his stick changed him back into a man. Having experienced sex as both man and woman, Tiresias sided with Jupiter, observing that women enjoy sex nine times more than men. Juno was so disgruntled with the answer that she struck him with blindness.[113] This punishment was too much for Jupiter. He couldn't undo Juno's divine punishment, but alleviated it by providing Tiresias with the ability to predict the future.

Tiresias's judgement seems to be confirmed by proverbs worldwide, that allude to fearsome female insatiability:

Water, fire and women will never say 'enough'. (Polish)

Women and fire: if you have to, take just a little. (Fulfulde, West Africa)

---

112   Riyad as-Salihin, *The Book of Miscellany*, كتاب المقدمات,
      Hadith 281
113   Ovid, *Metamorphoses*, Book III:82–83.

The man as long as he can, the woman as long as she
wants to. (Spanish, Bolivia)

The rat will die, and the hole will not be satisfied.
(Arabic, Tunisia)

Did the fear of female voraciousness result in female circumcision?
The Dogon people, an ethnic group indigenous to the central
plateau region of Mali, justify excision of the clitoris in the
following origin story, where the small 'potent' termite mound of
the Earth is not allowed to 'stand up' against the supreme male
creator and sky god:

> After Amma had created the Earth, he wanted to
> copulate with his partner. But the Earth had not yet
> been purified by excision, and the termite mound stood
> up against Amma. He cut it away and had sex with the
> Earth, while she was still bleeding from the wound.[114]

The mound literally rises up against male sexuality at the moment
of penetration and is considered a threat to the existing order.[115]

Cutting parts of male and female genitals have been presented
as taking away the 'remainders' of the other sex – for men, the
foreskin and for women, the clitoris – often including parts of
the labia as well. In myths that explain that women were once in
charge, the clitoris is sometimes referred to as a 'small penis'. It is

114 Marcel Griaule, *Dieu d'Eau*. (Fayard, 1966) p. 16.
115 Elisabeth Bekers, *Dissecting Anthills of W/Human Insurrection: A Comparative Study
     of African Creative Writing on Female Genital Excision*, 2002 p. 34. In the case of
     infibulation, the complete clitoris is cut off, along with all of the inner and much of
     the outer labia, followed by stitching up to close most of the vagina. Only a small
     opening is left for urine and menstrual blood. The friction caused by the artificially
     narrowed vagina increases male sexual pleasure.

likely that jealousy or fear of this little source of pleasure inspired the practice of female circumcision.

A reassuring order is established via surgical intervention intended to make girls 'completely feminine', to prevent them seeming like men. In rural areas in Egypt, rumours still prevail that the clitoris of an uncut girl will grow into a long penis. Removal of the androgynous part will 'purify' female genitals – just as the male foreskin is considered 'female' and must be circumcised.

Puberty rituals serve to symbolically separate boys from their mother's body, as initiation and circumcision inaugurate them into the secrets of the adult man's world. As their 'last bit of femininity' is cut away, the surrounding ceremony is meant to mark their 'second' or 'real' birth – the moment they become men, independent from their mothers.

The consequences of circumcision and excision, however, are completely different, physically as well as socially. Male circumcision 'unveils' the glans. The removal of the foreskin and the phallic exposure represents male licence to venture into the outside, non-domestic domain, whereas excision and infibulation of women's genitals leads to confinement and restriction.[116]

This difference in outcome is confirmed in proverbs worldwide, even in cultures without circumcision rituals. Expansive male spaces contrast with restricted female spaces. 'The home is the wife's world, the world is the man's home' is an Estonian saying. As for travelling, men should and women shouldn't. 'A son who never leaves home always thinks that his mother's is the loudest fart,' as a Kenyan Gikuyu proverb has it. Or, in a piece of Malaysian wisdom, 'A travelled woman is like a garden trespassed by cattle.'

---

116   Eric K. Silverman, *Anthropology and Circumcision* (Annual Review of Anthropology, 2004) p. 429.

The male need for hierarchy and control over women is confirmed in metaphors contrasting male expansion with female immobility. Open, outward male dynamic activities are set against closed, inward female realms. 'Woman' is equated with 'womb', 'house', and all that is 'inside' and needs to stay there, with the kitchen as dominion, and infibulation an extra lock on the womb to allow women to keep their good name.

The Quran condemns mutilation of the body and female genital cutting is not referred to anywhere. The Prophet Muhammad even emphasised women's right to be sexually satisfied. A few Hadith traditions claim that female genital cutting originated in the early Islamic world, but Islamic scholars have dismissed such statements as 'weak' and historically unsubstantiated: genital cutting existed long before Islam and was sometimes absorbed from local pre-Islamic traditions.

The Byzantine Greek physician and medical writer Aetius of Amida (sixth century CE) confirmed that the clitoris (*nymphê* in Greek) was removed when it became 'too large' or triggered arousal when rubbing against clothing. According to him, the Egyptians were inclined to remove a clitoris before it might grow too large, 'especially at that time when the girls were about to be married.' Aetius added accurate details on the procedure:

Have the girl sit on a chair while a muscled young man standing behind her places his arms below the girl's thighs. Have him separate and steady her legs and whole body. Standing in front and taking hold of the clitoris with a broad-mouthed forceps in his left hand, the surgeon stretches it outward, while with the right hand, he cuts it off at the point next to the pincers of the forceps. It is proper to let a length remain from that cut off, about the size of the membrane that's between

the nostrils, so as to take away the excess material only;
as I have said, the part to be removed is at that point just
above the pincers of the forceps. Because the clitoris is a
skin-like structure and stretches out excessively, do not
cut off too much, as a urinary fistula may result from
cutting such large growths too deeply.'[117]

The practice of infibulation, the ritual removal of the external
female genitalia and the suturing of the vulva, became linked
to slavery from the seventeenth century. In 1609 the Portuguese
missionary João dos Santos referred to a group near Mogadishu
who had a 'custome to sew up their Females, especially their
slaves being young to make them unable for conception, which
makes these slaves sell dearer, both for their chastitie, and for
better confidence which their Masters put in them.' Here, it is
clear that male control of the female body became 'associated
with shameful female slavery [and] came to stand for honour.'[118]

In nineteenth-century Europe and in the United States,
gynaecologists sometimes removed the clitoris of women to
prevent masturbation which was linked with perceived insanity.
The first Western clitoridectomy was carried out in 1822 in
Berlin on a fifteen-year-old girl who masturbated excessively.
The operation was described in *The Lancet* in 1825. There are
also nineteenth-century examples from England. This surgical
intervention was applied until the 1960s in the United States as a
treatment of hysteria, erotomania and lesbianism.[119]

---

117 Aetius quoted via Wikipedia, 'Female_genital_mutilation'; see also Mary Knight,
      Curing Cut or Ritual Mutilation? Some remarks on the practice of female and male
      circumcision in Graeco-Roman Egypt. *Isis*, 2001, 92 (2): 317–338.
118 Mackie, Gerry. 'Ending Footbinding and Infibulation: A Convention Account' in
      American Sociological Review. 61 (December 1996) (6) pp. 999–1017 (refs pp. 1003 and
      1009).
119 Sarah W. Rodriguez, 'Rethinking the History of Female Circumcision and

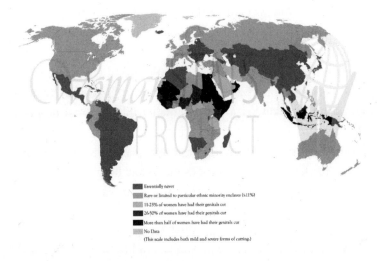

Essentially never
Rare or limited to particular ethnic minority enclaves (≤11%)
11-25% of women have had their genitals cut
26-50% of women have had their genitals cut
More than half of women have had their genitals cut
No Data
(This scale includes both mild and severe forms of cutting.)

Female genital mutilation rates by country, 2015.

More than 200 million women alive today have had to undergo clitoridectomy operations, mostly in Africa but also in some cultures in India and in Islamic countries like Yemen, Malaysia and more frequently, Indonesia.[120] Worries over virginity and nubility are used to justify female genital mutilation. A frequently used argument is that after the surgery a girl will be less likely to discredit family honour.

Usually it is the mothers, grandmothers and other female relatives who control the genital cutting of girls. The procedure creates a strong group identity. Social pressure makes it difficult for many women to leave their daughters uncut. Research

---

Clitoridectomy: American Medicine and Female Sexuality in the Late Nineteenth Century' in *Journal of the History of Medicine and Allied Sciences*. 63 (3), July 2008 pp. 323–347.

120 See statistics about female genital cutting online via Woman Stats; Kamran Paha in the *Huffington Post* 'Why Female Circumcision Violates Islam'.

indicates that the majority of mothers are determined to continue this tradition and apply it to their own daughters. The tradition is closely associated with ideas about purity, embedding in the community, sexuality and fertility.[121]

Since the second half of the twentieth century many people in the Western world have developed a strong awareness that the vagina and foreskin are a person's inalienable personal property. But this remains in conflict with traditional ideas that argue that the importance of genitals, foreskin, glans, clitoris and vulva reaches further than their owner's individual body.

What about masturbation? In most cultures the first aim of sex is procreation and stories rarely refer to masturbation. In the Bible the fact that Onan spilled his sperm on the earth 'was wicked in the sight of the Lord, and he put him to death' (Genesis 38:10) but masturbating girls or women are almost entirely absent in oral traditions. In myths I have found just one example: an African Adam and Eve story told in the Congolese province of Katanga. It comes from the *Jamaa* movement, an African sect rooted in Catholicism, and refers to 'playing with one's own body' with obvious disapproval. This oral Swahili story blames the original responsibility for all that has gone wrong between men and women on a conversation between Satan (here called Lucifer) and Eve. In summary, Eve goes for a walk in paradise when she hears the voice of Lucifer calling her from a tree. Feigning innocence, Lucifer asks Eve who she is and to whom her body belongs. Eve explains that her sex makes her female and her body belongs to her husband, as God told her right after

---

121   For some informative details, I made use of the nuanced article of Sandra. D. Lane and Robert A. Rubinstein, 'Judging the Other: Responding to Traditional Female Genital Surgeries', 1996 pp. 31–40. See also 'Forgotten Women: How one Kenyan woman escaped FGM and saved thousands more girls from the cut' by Lucy Anna Gray, *The Independent*, 21 January 2019.

he had created her: 'You are not a complete person; you will be
a complete person when you give your body to your husband so
that he may feel the beauty of your body. But if you play with it,
this will be your death.' However Lucifer convinces Eve that this
is a lie, and that by touching herself she can create new life:

> When Eve heard this she began to play with her body, all
> by herself. Her fecundity fell down on the ground. She
> saw it with her eyes. Now she began to feel shame and
> suffering and loneliness. She said to Lucifer: 'See what
> you did to me?' Lucifer laughed and went away quickly.
> Eve went back to her husband, silently, without saying
> anything and without asking for the body of Adam.
> And when Adam called her she wouldn't listen anymore.
> Adam thought, 'this woman has sinned, as God told us.'[122]

Masturbation does not contribute to the production of offspring –
an unacceptable outcome in societies where procreation is the main
purpose of life. God descends to the earth and punishes Adam and
Eve by depriving them of His love. From now on Adam and Eve
will need to buy each other's love by the sweat of their labour.[123]

Most origin stories in which female genitals play a role
reflect male awe and fear. The message is that sex is a dangerous
enterprise, but a man must produce offspring – and this holds
particularly true for the first man living in an otherwise empty
world. Heroic male courage is needed to overcome sexual threats.

As for the answer to the question raised by Jupiter and Juno,
disagreement continues to reign, while the 'little stone in the
vulva' keeps its own secret.

---

122   Fabian 1997: 1971: 124ff; also in Karin Barber: 27–28.
123   *Ibid.* 125.

Pre-Columbian earthenware pot.
Museo Larco, Lima

CHAPTER FIVE

POWERFUL BLOOD

That is the time when we are powerful and the men are afraid [...] woman, at her periods, is the vessel of a supernatural power, the power that allows her to give birth.[124]
(Tohono O'odham people, Arizona and Mexico)

They both got very angry. There was a big palaver. Finally, the man in his anger plucked a poisonous fruit which God had forbidden them to eat. He nearly swallowed it, but remembered in the last moment that the fruit was forbidden. So the fruit got stuck in his throat and can still be seen there. But the woman also plucked the fruit and she swallowed it. The fruit burst open her womb, and she began to bleed.[125]
(Igala, Nigeria)

---

124 Statement of a woman belonging to the Indian Tohono O'odham people in the Sonoran Desert, Arizona and Mexico, in Marta Weigle (1982) p. 173. Here, women were not considered unclean (as were menstruating women in a number of other cultures, e.g. in the Book of Leviticus in the Bible) but loaded with sacred power to take care of the growth of the clan.
125 In *Black Orpheus. A Journal of African and Afro-American Literature*, Vol. II, January 1958 p. 6.

BRIDAL TEXTS IN CUNEIFORM SCRIPT from more than 4,000 years ago address Inanna, Queen of Heaven, as female friends sing in honour of a young girl who is preparing for marriage:

> Now our breasts stand up!
> Now our parts have grown hair! Going to the bridegroom's loins […] Dance! Dance!
> Baba, let us be happy for our parts![126]

Baba was the pet name of Inanna, the Mesopotamian goddess of sex, love, war, justice and political power. Wedding songs were performed to Baba to bolster the confidence of inexperienced young – often child –brides.

Hymen, the god of marriage

Hymen is the Greek word for skin or membrane and also the name of the Greek god of marriage, most commonly held to be the son of Apollo and one of the Muses, or in some accounts the result of a coupling between Dionysus and Aphrodite. The anatomical usage originates from the idea of the vagina as a locked sanctuary of Aphrodite, the goddess of love, beauty, sexuality and fragility, who was also in charge of deflowering.

The hymen has traditionally been associated with virginity, as if it obstructed access to the vagina. That is not correct, because without an opening menstruation blood could not get out. A completely closed hymen would be an abnormality only to be fixed by surgical intervention. During childhood this thin

---

126   Thorkild Jacobsen, *The Harps That Once… Sumerian Poetry in Translation*, 1987 p. 18; cf. Zainab Bahrani, *Women of Babylon: Gender and Representation in Mesopotamia* (Routledge, 2001).

membrane begins to wear away due to sporting activities or masturbation, but often small remnants survive. The idea that the breaking of the hymen must be a painful experience for girls and an impossible task for boys has caused a lot of needless stress.

In communities where family honour is a crucial issue – and an intact hymen a must for brides – girls panic about not being able to convincingly prove their virginity. Traces of blood due to a presumed 'piercing' of the membrane during the wedding night must demonstrate that she had never 'done it' before. That is the reason why, in some traditions, both families still want to see bloodstained sheets as proof that the marriage has been consummated and the bride was indeed a virgin. A lack of bloodstains is interpreted as unchastity, which in some cultures may lead to repudiation or honour killing. A tragic and unnecessary drama, because the hymen of about half of all girls does not bleed during the first sexual experience. That is why medical doctors are unable to conclude from the state of the hymen whether a girl is a virgin or not.

In societies or groups with a virginity obsession, the demand for surgical reconstruction is huge – not just from brides, but also from prostitutes who can earn extra money as fake virgins. Considerably less complicated ways to suggest virginal loss of blood are the 'carmine pill' (a pill containing fake blood) that a woman can insert beforehand; a small finger cut; or the careful planning of menstruation with the help of the birth control pill.

Usually very little information is available about wedding night performances. Bridegrooms are warned that a girl may dread penetration; older men are aware that a young girl may feel reluctant or even abhorrent towards a man with whom she is going to share a life that others have decided for her. In proverbs, the husband is advised not to appear too delighted on the wedding night or in subsequent days, because it will make the young wife unbearably presumptuous:

> Neither praise the bride after the first night nor the shepherd after his first year. (Hebrew)

> A praised bride turns out to be a slob. (Farsi, Iran)

> If you love your wife, do not praise her before she is dead. (Bengal, Burmese, Czech, Russian)

A groom's fear can be no less overwhelming than the bride's: it is his duty, he has been taught, to deflower the bride on the wedding night. He must pierce the hymen, despite inexperience or advanced age. Do terrifying *vagina dentata* stories reflect male anguish around defloration? Sympathising with only his perspective, a Berber proverb laments: 'May God have mercy on the husband; as for the wife she knows what awaits her.'

Virginal bleeding

'The wind that opens the bedewed peach' is a poetic Chinese defloration image. 'Wind' refers to flirting here, but in combination with words invoking moisture or rain it carries more direct sexual connotations.[127] In some cultures the hymen is deliberately ruptured in the first days of a baby's life by the mother herself, for reasons of exaggerated cleanliness or because the girl is being prepared for premature intercourse with adult

---

127   Barnard Wolfe, *The Daily Life of a Chinese Courtesan Climbing up a Tricky Ladder: with A Chinese Courtesan's Dictionary*, 1980 p. 18.

men. Among the Sakalava in Madagascar, girls would break their
own hymen before marriage, if their parents hadn't already seen
to it. No reason at all for the groom to worry.[128]

There are also traditions in which the hymen was considered
so dangerous that it drastically impeded enjoyment. In Vedic
texts the blood of the wedding night was presented as poisonous
and the virginal vagina as a seat of danger.[129] Although male
fear of deflowering a girl does not exist everywhere, some
inexperienced grooms still prefer to leave that acid test to
someone else:

> [...] someone immune to its dangers – a woman
> perhaps, using an instrument; or, paradoxically, a person
> ordinarily taboo, such as a close relative, a brother or
> father; or, sometimes, a priest, may rupture the hymen.[130]

Ancient texts point out that, among the Phoenicians, a special
slave was commissioned for the task of deflowering. Jehan de
Mandeville (a.k.a. Sir John Mandeville), the fourteenth-century
writer of a widely read fictional travel journal, suggests that on
a particular oriental island a small group of men committed
themselves to the precarious business of deflowering girls:

> Then you come to an island where is the custom, if one
> takes a wife, he does not sleep with her as the first man,
> but there are poor servants who do this and take the
> girl's virginity, and for doing so the servants are paid...
> The vagina of the daughters is sorcered and poisoned,

---

128 Ploss and Bartels, 1912 pp. 209–210.
129 Verrier, *Myths of Middle* India, 1949 p. 365.
130 More examples in Lederer:44; Freud, 'Das Tabu der Virginität' in *Gesammelte Werke*
     XII:161.

that it is dangerous to sleep with a daughter for the first time, but later on it is not dangerous at all.[131]

Perhaps the greatest surprise is that this task was performed by 'poor servants'. In most examples from India and South America, it is chiefs or priests who service the new brides.

Even in places where little attention is paid to the hymen, such as New Caledonia, some men would refuse to deflower their own wives, preferring to rent for that task a *perceur attitré* (an official penetrator) as the French observer Léon Moncelon noted in the nineteenth century.

Ritual defloration woodcut in *Les Voyages de Jehan de Mandeville*. Strasbourg, 1484 edition.

According to the ancient Greek historian Herodotus (484–424 BCE), the North African Nasamones, living in the area that is now southeast Libya, had a particular custom of their own.

---

131   *Les Voyages de Jehan de Mandeville* was probably written in 1356. Quoted in Jörg Wettlaufer, who provides more examples in his article, 'The *jus primae noctis* as a Male Power Display' in *Evolution and Human Behaviour*, Vol. 1, 2 (March, 2000) p. 116.

In their tradition, during the course of the wedding night, the bride was obliged to have intercourse with every male guest, who had to give her a present each in return. This male solidarity was indispensable not only to undo the power of a single hymen and to satisfy the violated bride, but also to placate the spirits whose task was to defend the young woman against intruders. Such a ritual serial rape served to dilute the dangerous supernatural power released during the tearing of the hymen, by spreading the risk among all the men.[132]

Other traditions, on the contrary, presented the defloration of a young girl as a particular honour or special gift offered to a god. In ancient Rome, 'The Roman bride sat down on the lap of the god Mutunus, so that his phallus entered her vagina, tore the hymen apart and widened the vagina.'[133] Similar ceremonies exist in India. In Kanara on the western coast, and also around Goa, such sacrifices are conducted. Before they marry, girls go to the temple and offer the 'firstlings' of marriage to a statue of Shiva with an iron lingam and this God takes delivery of the 'sacrifice'.[134]

The right to this offering was also bestowed upon a priest as the god's representative, acting as a divine deputy. An illustration in a Persian Islamic manuscript from 1602 shows a Christian priest busy deflowering a young bride before the groom has access to her. The young woman is lying on her back with a pillow under her head. The lower part of her body is naked and the priest is moving between her thighs. The groom, dressed in a Christian outfit (marked with yellow patches, according to Islamic prescriptions) is patiently waiting outside until the priestly treatment is finished. According to the author

---

132   Herodotus, *Histories*, Book 4 pp. 172–173.
133   Ploss and Bartels p. 211.
134   *Ibid.*

of the manuscript, Muhammad Al-Qazwini, this was a typical Christian custom.[135]

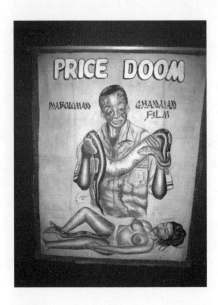

Ghanaian film poster.

Such examples of practical or ritual defloration – by the mother, a divine statue, a priest, a family member, a slave, a servant or a foreigner – were often inspired by paranoid fear of the magic powers or poisonous effects of hymenal blood. They had nothing to do with the so-called *jus primae noctis* ('right to the first night'), a medieval privilege often postulated as a *droit du seigneur* or the lord of the manor's right to have sexual intercourse with a vassal's bride on her wedding night. This right was also referred to as *droit de cuissage* (literally, 'a right to the thighs'); or in a free translation can be interpreted as the right of powerful men to have sex at will.

135   This Persian manuscript of 1602 is a translation of an Arabic work by Zakariya al-Qazwini (1203–83 CE) in the collection of Leiden University Libraries, with thanks to Dr Karin Scheper.

The first literary example of this presumed right dates to around 1900 BCE in the Mesopotamian *Epic of Gilgamesh*. In that text, it is evident that Gilgamesh, as King of Uruk, is entitled to have sex with every betrothed woman or bride before any other man has access to her. In his *Histories*, Herodotus goes on to describe the Adyrmachidae, another tribe in Libya, where custom demanded that all girls who wanted to marry had to first visit the king, who had the right to deflower them all. The medieval Vikings also assumed this right in Irish monasteries where they overpowered Christian brides-to-be.[136] To this day, contemporary rulers and other powerful men continue to claim this right, with differing degrees of approbation and censure.

Scholars seem to disagree whether medieval landlords literally shared the bed with the virgin brides of their workers. The ancient rituals inspired by male anguish about deflowering a girl are largely replaced here by the hierarchical reasoning: 'Owing to my status, I have a right to your body.' Perhaps their powerful position gave them the reckless feeling that they were personally immune to the hymen danger. In his book *Chimpanzee Politics*, Frans de Waal compares modern-day equivalents to 'alpha males' among primates. A male of high status, in competition with his peers, will clock up more copulations and produce more offspring. In industrialised societies, life turns less on reproduction than on sexual prestige within one's group. Across cultural traditions, men have thought up rules by which their privileges regarding their sexual 'rights to women' are assured.

From my Congo years, I remember that wherever President Mobutu Sese Seko deigned to visit, young girls had to dance for him. *Nomen est omen* in this case: the name he chose for himself by decree, *Mobutu Sese Seko Nkuku Ngbendu Wa Za Banga* means

---

136   155. Cf. Wettlaufer.

'The all-powerful warrior who, because of his endurance and inflexible will to win, goes from conquest to conquest, leaving fire in his wake.' The president was accustomed to select one or more of these dancing girls to have sex with. I am not sure that the family concerned considered it a great honour to have their young daughter deflowered by the nation's highest chief, as David Van Reybrouck suggests in his book *Congo*. I remember a friend's consternation after Mobutu sent her a preciously ornamented belt, signifying that the president had a more than ordinary interest in her. For her own security she had to leave the country in haste, because the chief knows his rights: no one dares refuse him anything.

Other dangers beyond a sorcerous, poisonous or mortal hymen loom on a wedding night. Some communities warn against the risk of conceiving a child on the night of defloration. If the very first coitus results in a pregnancy, the mighty hymenal blood will result in the birth of a sick or handicapped child. Unfortunately, the fear of female blood is not restricted to hymenal bleeding. In many cultures, blood originating from a female body has been associated directly with danger for the community in general and for men in particular. This holds especially true for menstrual blood.

Myths about menstruation

Every culture refers to the first menstruation in its own way. In Japan it is depicted as 'the year of the splitting melon'; among the Xhosa, the 'unbudding of the flower'; in Germany, as the beginning of the 'monthly flower' and in India as 'the five arrows of the god of love'.[137] Origin myths explain the beginning of this mysterious bleeding and its consequences, connecting it to monthly rules

---

137   Ploss and Bartels p. 169.

and prohibitions with both positive and negative connotations. In an Egyptian funerary text (eighteenth to sixteenth century BCE), the colour red is associated with hostile forces and cosmic battles in the process of creation – although it is not quite clear whether it is the woman herself or her menstrual bleeding that was disapproved of.[138]

In stories that do not present menstruation as a punishment, the explanation postulated for this natural phenomenon is completely different. In a Saramo story from Tanzania, for example, the bleeding is due to an accidental disfigurement:

Long, long ago, there were only two men, who lived on honey. One of the men climbed a tree. The bees had built a nest up there and he wanted to get the honey from inside the tree with his axe. Suddenly the sharp blade of the axe fell down and hit the other man, who was lying on his back asleep right there under that tree. The falling axe hit his penis and cut it off. What was left was a bleeding wound like women have.

His companion climbed down and asked, 'What is that?'

'The axe cut it off,' he replied.

Then they slept together and a girl was born. They slept together again and a boy was born. A world of people descended from those two men. Ever since then, women lose blood down there, just like that first woman. (Saramo, Tanzania)[139]

---

138 O'Rourke: 'The Wt-Woman' in *Zeitschrift für Ägyptische Sprache und Altertumskunde*, Vol. 134, 2 (2007), pp. 170–171.

139 Otto Dempwolff, 'Märchen der Zalamo und Hehe in Deutsch Ost-Afrika' in *Anthropophyteia* (9) 1904 pp. 396–397.

In a dramatic turn of events, a mutilated man becomes the first woman, who spontaneously starts bleeding from her fresh wound and is soon able to give birth to the very first children. No question of punishment here.

In a Koya story from Andhra Pradesh, India, there were women from the beginning, but they never bled. But as a consequence, babies were born without eyes or mouths and quickly died. The population did not grow – a worrisome situation. So one of the ancestors, Sukra Koya, went to consult Deur (God):

> Deur asked him, 'Do women have a flow of blood every month?'
>
> 'No,' he said, 'I have never heard of that.'
>
> Deur plucked a leaf and gave it to Sukra: 'Pound up this leaf and put it in the place where people fetch water. All the unmarried girls will get a flow of blood. It will frighten them at first, but you must explain things to them and teach them how to bathe at the end of their time and boil their clothes in a new pot.'
>
> Moreover, Deur said, 'On the third day after the first bath, tell the girls to make a doll of grass. They must blacken the doll with charcoal and then take it with a hen's egg to a crossroads. There they must sacrifice a fowl in my name and bury the doll and the egg.'[140]

The Koya did as Deur had advised, and from then on all ended well as far as healthy progeny was concerned. In other Koya stories a fruit or vegetable provokes the first menstruation among

---

140   Elwin 1954 pp. 475–476.

the first foremothers.[141] The message is simply that menstruation is part of a healthy life.

Other traditions have a different view of the matter, and the first menstruation is presented as a punishment for a woman's first grave infringement in the early days of mankind: 'Abuse came from your mouth, blood will flow from your vulva.' [...] Since that day women have had a period of blood-flowing every month.' (Bondo, India).[142]

In Judaism, Christianity and Islam, stories and comments abound presenting menstruation as a well-deserved punishment. In various rabbinic stories Eve menstruates for the first time after she has slept with the archangel of death Samael or the Serpent, who opened the source, 'and this is how the flood of impurity and the monthly female illness have come into the world.'[143]

Satan smartly turns God's commandment upside down in a Javanese Islamic story: he fools Eve by telling her that she will only be chased from paradise if she does not eat the forbidden *khuldi* fruit. Since there are only two such fruits, Eve immediately swallows one. It gives her such immense pleasure that she falls down and faints. Then right away she starts bleeding, and because 'she did not remember the divine prohibition of eating the *khuldi* fruit, all women lose blood during the monthly periods.'[144]

Neither in the Genesis story in the Bible nor in the Quran is there any reference to menstruation as a punishment for Eve eating the forbidden fruit, but various interpreters reinforce the hierarchical relations between men and women by imposing punitive sanctions on male contact with an 'unclean' woman. The belief that menstruation was impure resulted in detailed

---

141   *Ibid.*
142   Elwin 1949 p. 274.
143   Eisenmenger, *Natursagen*, (1711) 1907 p. 211.
144   Steenbrink p. 118.

prescriptions in the Hebrew Bible: 'When a woman has a discharge, and the discharge in her body is blood, she shall be in her menstrual impurity for seven days, and whoever touches her shall be unclean until the evening' (Leviticus 15:19).

The Quran (2:222) also advises men to stay away from women as long as they are 'impure', without making a connection between menstruation and the violation of God's commandment. But Quran scholar Tabari (839–923) considers Eve's first menstruation as a punishment for making the tree in paradise bleed by eating its fruit. The work of Sahih al-Bukhari, considered by Islamic scholars as the most authentic book after the Quran, associates lack of intelligence, a female shortcoming since Eve, with menstruation:

Once Allah's Apostle [...] passed by [a group of] women and said, 'O women! Give alms, as I have seen that the majority of the dwellers of Hellfire were you (women).'

They asked, 'Why is it so, O Allah's Apostle?' He replied, 'You curse frequently and are ungrateful to your husbands. I have not seen anyone more deficient in intelligence and religion than you. A cautious sensible man could be led astray by some of you.' The women asked, 'O Allah's Apostle! What is deficient in our intelligence and religion?' He said, 'Is not the evidence of two women equal to the witness of one man?' They replied in the affirmative. He said, 'This is the deficiency in her intelligence. Isn't it true that a woman can neither pray nor fast during her menses?' The women replied in the affirmative. He said, 'This is the deficiency in your religion.'[145]

---

145 Sahih al-Bukhari Book 6, Hadith 304.

In the Quran there is no association between menstruation and intelligence, and nor did I find it elsewhere.

In Christianity, the presumed uncleanness of the first foremother (and all women after her) formed a stark contrast with the 'unstained purity' of the Virgin Mary. The Catholic Church still sticks to the doctrine that Mary was a lifelong virgin with an intact hymen despite giving birth, and never menstruated.[146]

Oral stories go into the details of the first people's bodily changes after the eating of the forbidden fruit – in which Adam gets a better deal than Eve. In the Igala story quoted at the start of this chapter, and in various other traditions, Eve swallowed the fruit in a hurry and began to bleed, whereas Adam reacted hesitantly, and the forbidden fruit got stuck in his throat, and that's where man's Adam's apple comes from.

Some Islamic variants of the Adam and Eve story still serve as proof of Eve's hypersensitivity to Satan's arguments. In Turkish rural communities, the eating of the forbidden fruit is explained as a sign of women's moral weakness, the very reason why women must be supervised by men. Girls are taught that the female body is repulsive and needs to be carefully hidden. Even though men may sometimes lose blood – while hunting, in a war or in an accident – for them the loss of blood is incidental. Men are independent, they master their blood and their sperm, while women leak blood and milk from their bodies uncontrollably.[147] Such reasoning converts physical differences into justification of a hierarchical order.

---

146 Ranke-Heinemann p. 21.
147 Carol Delaney, 'Mortal Flow: Menstruation in Turkish Village Society' in *Blood Magic*, 1988 pp. 79 and 82.

Monthly magic

A disadvantage can be turned into an advantage, as we learn from
a note written by Pliny the Elder (23 or 24–79 CE), who believed
that a naked menstruating woman would suppress whirlwinds,
hailstorms and lightning. If, in her monthly state, she walked
around a field, caterpillars, beetles and other vermin would
spontaneously fall from the ears of corn.[148]

This does not prevent many cultures from associating contact
with a menstruating woman with entirely negative connotations.
Her bleeding would weaken hunters and warriors, kill young
plants, sour wines, putrefy meat, curdle milk, and the horse's back
on which she sat would break. In many communities she was
forced to pass her 'unclean' days in isolation.[149]

Numerous rules have been invented to limit the perceived
damage caused by menstruation. In the ultra-orthodox Jewish
tradition, the appearance of a menstruating woman in public would
cause disasters: her blood prevents bread from rising and damages
the harvest. And according to medieval Jewish mystic sources, 'God
abandons menstruants because God cannot suffer impurity.'[150] The
ancient Greeks believed that menstruating women would make
the land barren, the mirrors they looked in turned opaque and sex
during a period made them pregnant with snakes. In parts of Japan
and among some Amerindian peoples, women were obliged to stay
away from cattle and were not allowed to touch people's food. A

---

148   As explained in the work of his nephew Pliny the Younger, *Historia Naturalis*, xxviii.
      Chapter 23, in John Bostock's *Pliny the Elder* web edition.
149   Peggy Reeves Sanday, *Female Power and Male Dominance: On the Origin of Sexual
      Inequality*, (Cambrdige University Press, 1988), Chapter 5; Eloïse Mozzani, *Le Livre des
      Superstitions: Mythes, Croyances et Légendes*, (Robert Laffont, 1995) 512ff. For the search
      of a cultural balance during the mighty flowing of blood, see the work Mary Douglas.
150   Sharon Faye Koren, *Forsaken: The Menstruant in Medieval Jewish Mysticism.*
      Lebanon: Brandeis University Press, 2011.

North Siberian belief held that during menstruation women should not look up at the sky, since the sky represents purity. In Europe, a stubborn rumour circulated that sex with a menstruating woman would cause male impotence or other disasters such as baldness. As soon as an Australian Aboriginal discovered that his menstruating wife had been lying on his blanket, he killed her on the spot, and within a fortnight he himself died of sheer terror.[151]

Among the Ila in Zambia there was a belief that a man would lose his manhood by eating with a menstruating woman. She was not allowed to touch pots and pans and had to stay away from the common cooking fire. In some cultures, women were set apart in a menstruation hut and not allowed to eat food that had been declared taboo for them – usually the most appreciated and healthiest dishes such as meat or fish. In Winnebago belief, sacred objects would lose their power in contact with a menstruating woman, and even ghosts would not survive contact. So many rules have been invented worldwide to combat women's monthly bleeding that Briffault, in his three-volume book *The Mothers* (1927), devoted twenty-five pages to the topic, with the modest mention that his elaborate list was far from complete. It is worth noting that some of these beliefs still exist in remote areas.

Briefly summarised, the most frequent restrictions on women during their periods, are:

1. Sex is not allowed.
2. Menstruating women must take into consideration limitations regarding dress, eating, movement and contact with things or people.
3. Menstruating women are not permitted to touch male ritual equipment or weaponry.

---

151 Briffault's examples (1927) are referred to in Lederer, Chapter 4.

4. Menstruating women are not allowed to prepare or cook food.
5. Menstruating women are set apart in special huts.[152]

Such rules turned out differently in practice than originally intended. There is no single or absolute menstrual taboo, and taboos surrounding the menstrual cycle may well have restricted the behaviour of other people more than the menstruating woman herself. Women certainly made smart use of the rules by shifting the blame for family disasters on menstruating co-wives or by frightening a husband to death with the threat of mixing drops of menstrual blood in his food. Anxiety and negative attention to female periods from women as well as men have promoted hierarchical relationships and apartheid of the sexes.

Menstrual blood was believed to be dangerously powerful, and menstruation was one of the most baffling enigmas for people to explain. In many cultures women themselves internalised the importance of their monthly seclusion. They would never risk exposing the family and the community to its negative effects, even to the point of perceiving themselves as seriously harmful and dangerous during menstruation. In some Amerindian cultures, women exploited the authority that menstrual bleeding afforded them, arguing that this was 'the time when we are powerful and the men are afraid'.[153] In southern Portugal women derived special powers from menstruation, even though some believed – up until the late 1970s – that these powers were beyond their own control: plants withered away and objects started moving as soon as a menstruating woman came close. In that region women tell a story about São Bras (Saint Blaise or Blasius), the only male

---

152 Briffault in Lederer, ibid.; Robert H. Lowie, *Primitive Religion*, 1925:211ff; Reeves Sanday 1988 p. 104.
153 Mary Douglas 1975 pp. 62–63; Marta Weigle 1982 pp. 171–173.

saint to be carried around on a local holy day. In churches he is depicted with striking red hands, which he sustained as a result of indiscreet behaviour long before he was canonised. Driven by sexual passion in his youth, he had groped a young menstruating woman, and when he took his hands away from under her skirts, they were covered in blood. Since then, São Bras devoted his life to good works, but his hands remained blood-red to remind him and others of the reprehensible behaviour of his youth. This Blasius story is a local version of the life story of the Armenian physician, bishop and canonised martyr.[154]

In Greek and Roman antiquity as well as in the Jewish tradition there was a taboo on sex with menstruating women. Pliny the Elder, and many scholars after him, insisted that sex with a menstruating woman was dangerous. In the first century, Jewish-Greek scholar Philo of Alexandria banned sex with menstruating women because menstrual blood would keep the womb moist and thereby damage the vitality of male seed. Sex was only meant to produce offspring, according to the reasoning of that time. It was already known that during monthly periods nothing could be begotten, so what was the point anyway? Christianity adopted the existing prohibition without critical reflection.

Jews and Christians alike quoted threateningly from the book of Leviticus (20: 18): 'If a man lies with a woman having her sickness, and uncovers her nakedness, and she has uncovered the fountain of her blood; both of them shall be cut off from among their people.' Some translations upgrade 'cut off' to 'exterminated'. An explanation for this merciless punishment might be that religious Jews as well as many non-Jews were convinced that menstrual blood was toxic.[155]

---

154 Denise L. Lawrence, 'Menstrual Politics: Women and Pigs in Rural Portugal' in *Blood Magic*: 117–136.
155 Ranke-Heinemann 1990 p. 21.

Whether or not under classical influence, some church fathers were certain that children born sick or disabled were the result of sex during menstruation. The most frequently mentioned diseases or abnormalities were leprosy, hydrocephalus, epilepsy, paralysis, crossed eyes, crooked legs, a hump or insanity. From the fifteenth century, the idea that disabled babies were born due to conceiving during menstruation lost its persuasiveness. Still, some Christian theologians kept those frightening ideas in play for their believers through the ages – here and there even into the twentieth century.[156]

Initially, the early church distinguished itself from surrounding cultures by asserting equality between men and women, but sooner or later, male church scholars excluded women from the liturgy and the holy altar on the basis of 'monthly impurity'. And in the Catholic Church women are still not allowed to be priests. In various traditions menophobia, the fear of menstrual blood is still deployed to keep women away from certain positions. Fear of the polluting presence of menstruating women was and is strongest in societies where men feel that their authority is at risk: they feel compelled to avoid women's blood and other dangerous female substances as much as possible. In the event of contamination, they desperately try to eliminate the harmful effect by any means.

Male menstruation

The widespread belief in the dangers of menstrual blood continued to intrigue those who did not have the experience, so it is not altogether surprising that according to some myths, in the beginning menstruation was a man's business:

---

156   For detailed clerical Catholic ideas about menstruation, cf. Ranke-Heinemann, part II.

Long ago things were different from now: the women had beards and moustaches and the men had something small inside their bodies, it looked like a shell and it contained a living creature. Every month that creature caused them to bleed. Their wives had no such flow of blood, but for the men this was very inconvenient. For some days every month they had to stop carrying out chores such as cutting wood or working in the fields. It was too risky for them to go outside at the time of blood, because the tigers smelled it and ate them immediately.

One day there was a marriage and everyone prepared to go to the wedding festivities. A young wife said to her husband, 'Why don't you take my beard and moustache for a change and give me your little shell? I would love to see what it feels like to have blood flowing from me.' He agreed and so it happened that the girl stuck her beard and moustache on her husband's face and she fitted his shell with the living creature into her own body.

After the wedding they tried to return the things they had exchanged, but the hair had stuck to the man's face and the shell could not be removed from the girl's inside. 'It is not too bad,' the girl said. 'I can now get plenty of cloth, because I need at least seven layers to cover my parts. And also, my husband looks very handsome with that beard.' She went out and when the other women touched her, they too began to bleed and from then on, all women have a monthly period.[157] (Halba, India)

---

157   Elwin, 1949 p. 240.

Here, the bleeding is not a matter of guilt or punishment. Various Eastern European stories also imagine how, in the beginning, God imposed the menstrual period on Adam and the male gender. So in ancient times men had blood flowing from their knees every month – or from a body part that went unnamed for reasons of prudishness – but they did not know how to deal with menstruation or with other 'women's issues' such as cleaning, cooking or giving birth, so God reversed the roles. Such stories are told by women with great enthusiasm to confirm that men are unable to cope with traditional female roles.

In a number of cultures, initiation rites of boys during puberty served to reverse the malignant effect of female blood that contaminated all men during their birth from the mother's body. A boy receives an incision in the tongue at the start of puberty – an operation that causes bleeding, just like a girl's first menstrual period. The tongue is deemed to have been seriously polluted by the mother's milk he drank from the day of his birth. With the incision, he is safely released from all the pernicious female elements and influences he gulped down during his childhood.[158]

In Melanesian and Australian cultures, the belief in and fear of the malignant influence of female menstrual and birth blood developed from the fact that men and women were considered interdependent. Both sexes were weakened by the 'contaminating' effect of sex, but the woman has an advantage because her monthly bleeding relieves her of the contagion, whereas recurrent contact with women weakens men further and further.

In his book *The Island of Menstruating Men*, Ian Hogbin describes the reasoning that the people of Wogeo (an island off the north coast of Papua New Guinea) developed about female uncleanness in their society: women are naturally inferior but can

---

158   More examples and details in Bettelheim, 1954:167ff.

be dangerous during menstruation. A Wogeo man has the right to beat his wife, but in doing so he takes a risk: at her next period, she can touch his food and cause him a fatal illness.

When a Wogeo boy starts having sex, he must initiate his own 'period'. He first catches a lobster and removes one of the claws, which he keeps with ginger in a leaf until the day set for the bleeding, on which day he fasts. He undresses on a lonely beach, wades into the water up to his knees, sets his legs apart and as soon as he gets an erection, pushes the foreskin back and cuts the glans with the lobster claw, first on the left and then on the right. When the wound begins to dry up and the seawater no longer turns red, he walks back to the beach where he wraps his penis in leaves. He is not allowed to have sex until the next new moon.

For those who believe in it, this operation has the desired effect: after the bleeding the boy's body glows with energy and self-confidence. It is also the custom for warriors to take a bleeding before they go on a raid; for traders, before carving out a canoe for an overseas trip; and for hunters, before weaving a new net to catch wild pigs. The men have created their own successful menstrual rituals to deflect from the harmful influences of female blood.[159]

Of the worldwide list of disasters said to be caused by menstruating women, we may hope that most have now been reduced to footnotes in local cultural history. An old family anecdote from the southern United States provides a simple recipe for women who worry that their loved one might run away – just put 'a spoonful of your "time of the month" in his coffee regularly,' and he'll never leave you. The proof is delivered at the end of the story: 'Your uncle died in your aunt's arms and loved her to his last breath.'[160]

---

159   Ian Hogbin, *The Island of Menstruating Men*, 1970:96ff.
160   Matthew Kirksey, quoted in *Blood Magic* p. 35.

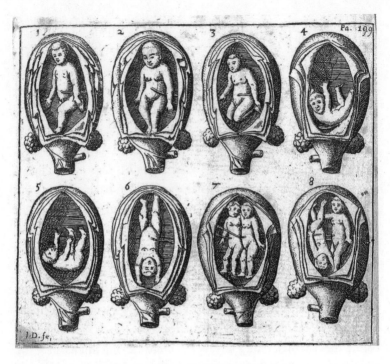

Foetuses in various positions. Jane Sharp, *The Midwives Book*, 1671.

CHAPTER SIX

A STOREHOUSE BENEATH THE NAVEL

She who leaves a child behind, lives eternally.
(Chagga, Tanzania)

The woman who has a storehouse beneath the navel,
will never die of hunger or cold.
(Sephardic, Spain/Portugal)

IN CONGO, I asked my all-male first-year students to write an essay about 'the purpose of life'. They agreed almost unanimously that having children was far and away the most important part of life. During our discussions it turned out that their biggest fear was that their future wife's storehouse would be locked. Men can, of course, be infertile too, but the blame was firmly laid on the women.

Fertility and pregnancy are praised in all cultures. In proverbs, a childless woman is harshly compared to a tent without tent pegs (Ladino), a day without sun (Czech), a cow without a bell (German), a tree without birds (Thai), a solitary flower on a mountain top (Vietnamese), and so forth.

In stories, childless women desperately look for a solution to their disastrous lack:

> [They] fell pregnant as soon as they were in the vicinity of certain places: rocks, caves, trees or rivers. The infant souls entered their bodies and they fell pregnant. Whether these infant souls were the souls of ancestors or not, one thing was certain: they had been waiting all this time to become human, hidden in crevices or cavities, in pools or forests. They had already led some kind of embryonic life in the womb of their real Mother, the Earth.[161]

The Earth was where children came from, which is why nineteenth-century Europeans believed children were brought by aquatic animals – fish or frogs – or by birds, especially storks.

Miraculous pregnancy

Miraculous conceptions are of all times and cultures. Storytellers explore human anatomy and life-creating powers with curiosity. A Baniwa story from Brazil has the first woman falling pregnant when she gently pressed a stick against her cheek. In their desire to fall pregnant, some women look for help in extraordinary places, others in certain drinks or food. Or they meet a spirit or an angel before a child comes to life inside them. Unusual conceptions reflect the enduring human wonder at the coming into existence of new life.[162]

---

161 Mircea Eliade, *Myths, Dreams and Mysteries*, (Harper Collins, 1960) pp. 164–165.
162 Weigle: 86ff.

Sometimes the stars are invoked, or the sun or the moon, the wind or lightning, ancestors or symbols of power. Offerings are made to a wide range of entities. Sometimes it's a question of coming into contact with a special footprint in stone or rock, supposedly from Adam or Buddha, from Ali (Muhammad's son-in-law) or the Christian saint Thomas.

A Chinese woman who saw a huge human footprint wanted a son of the same impressive proportions:

> The woman stood still where the Supreme God had left an imprint of his big toe and at that moment, at that spot, she felt how her core was seized and – filled with deep religious wonderment – she realised she was pregnant.[163]

There are innumerable stories about people connecting with the powers of stone: stones are solid, they do not die, whereas mankind is mortal. No wonder young women let their bodies slide over stones or must jump over a whole row of fertility stones to fall pregnant. In the French city of Rennes there are stones known as *pierres des épousées* or *pierres marieuses* that are sought out by brides-to-be for their powers of marital bliss. Near Verdun there is a rock known as the 'Armchair of Saint Lucie', where the saint was said to have left an imprint of her body and women who wish to become pregnant should simply sit on the chair.

Among Muslims, a similar idea is found near Tunis, at the famous tomb of Sidi Fethalla. Childless women go there, risking their lives as the climb is steep and slippery. Some even do so repeatedly. On Saturday, this holy man's day, they first invoke him and then rub a flat stone on their bellies.

---

163   P. Saintyves, *Les vierges mères*, 1908:22ff.

As well as stones enhancing fertility, there are rivers, lakes and springs endowed with the same effect. You can drink their special water or immerse yourself in it. A spring can make women fall pregnant after a benevolent god has added a few drops of sperm to its waters.[164]

The importance of fertility is magnified in impressive shrines, for example, in Hindu culture. Infertile women pray mostly to Shiva, the god of creative power and fertility. His emblem is the lingam, which can be found on street corners or in temples, in the form of a standing stone. In the southern Indian city of Thanjavur, a famous temple dedicated to Shiva, more than a thousand years old, boasts an 8.7-metre-high lingam, one of the largest in the world. Lingams come in all sizes, they are rubbed with special oil, covered with flowers and perfume, offered sacrifices, and people prostrate themselves in front of them. Infertile women spend a night in the temple in a special room reserved for them. There, in the dark, they are visited by Shiva. The inner part of the temple, the holy of holies, is called *karuvarai*, the Tamil word for 'womb room', with *karu* meaning foetus.[165] In many rituals a simple touch suffices. In short, there are a striking number of stories about pregnancy in which men play no role at all.

In several origin stories there were just women at the beginning of time, or countries where only women lived and managed fine without men, and we are told how pregnancy came about in these communities. In India and Taiwan, it is said that the women were fertilised by hornets or by the bulging navels some women had, or that they pleasured themselves or each other with wooden organs.

The wind was also believed to be a powerful fertiliser, although some variants specify that only a storm could have the desired

---

164   Many examples in Mircea Eliade, Naissances Mystiques.
165   More examples in Saintyves.

effect. It happened this way – the woman who wanted to fall pregnant climbed a mountain or stood on a roof, bent over, lifted her skirt, and the wind blew around her vulva, causing a child to spontaneously grow in her belly. Prevailing male perspectives commented with clear disapproval on such imaginary female communities. Their accounts are tinged with fear – not least of being superfluous to the impregnation process. These women were said to be man-haters, they wept whenever a baby boy was born instead of a girl; or they would immediately kill all male babies they gave birth to. Those poor little boys were torn apart or had boiling water poured over them. And these are just a few of many more dreadful scenarios.[166]

Male apprehension about such stories is expressed in contradictory ways. First, in a warning against unconstrained female power aimed at destroying men – just look how they exterminate baby boys! Second, in a boundless need to belittle women – of course, they cannot survive all by themselves, without men; the girls they give birth to are degenerate and worthless, and these women are unfit to give birth to a healthy baby boy; women who masturbate with a wooden penis will only produce children without bones, who won't survive for more than a few days. No, sturdy male offspring require real male potency. There is an unstable balance between female birth-giving and male attainment and assumptions of power. It is quite human to debunk a fearful obsession by inventing a more reassuring version of events.

---

166   e.g. Lederer p. 105.

Male input

The idea that only the mother produces a child is probably the oldest. However, over time the male contribution has been greatly magnified, in line with the emergence of patriarchal societies. This development is reflected in both myths and in literary texts. The *Eumenides* (451 BCE) was the final part of a trilogy of tragedies called the *Oresteia*, written by the Greek playwright Aeschylus. They were performed together during the annual Dionysos Festival in Athens. In the *Eumenides*, Orestes is being chased by the Furies, the revenge goddesses, after he kills his mother Clytemnestra. Apollo stands up for him:

> The mother of what is called her child, is no parent of
> it, but nurse only of the young life that is sown in her.
> [...] The parent is the male, and she but the stranger,
> a friend, who, if fate spares his plant, preserves it till it
> puts forth.[167]

This belief is of Egyptian origin, according to historian Diodorus of Sicily (c. 90–30 BCE) who observed that the 'Egyptians hold the father alone to be the author of generation, and the mother only to provide a nest and nourishment for the foetus.'[168]

It is relevant here to go back for a moment to the domain of the Greek gods, a divine world where female anatomy was not needed for procreation. In his work on the origin of the gods, the writer Hesiod (mid eighth century BCE) called Metis, the main adviser to the supreme god Zeus and mother to his daughter Athena, wiser than all other gods and humans. However, after the

---

167   Aeschylos, *Eumenides*, lines 657–661, quoted in Needham: 25.
168   *Ibid*.

prophecy that the king of the gods would lose his power to his second child, Earth and Heaven advised Zeus to swallow Metis when she became pregnant: only then would his power remain superior to all immortal gods. Fearing the loss of his lightning-hurling superiority, Zeus grasped Metis with both hands and wolfed her down.

From within, Metis continued to generously provide him with wise advice, and in due course Zeus himself gave birth to a daughter – bright-eyed Athena. The blacksmith Hephaestus cleaved Zeus' skull and Athena leaped from her father's head fully armed, or in Hesiod's words:

> [...] the awful, the strife-stirring, the host-leader, the unwearying, the queen, who delights in tumults and wars and battles [...] a fearsome queen who brings the sound of war and, tirelessly, leads the host.[169]

Eileithyia, goddess of childbirth, assisting Zeus at the birth of Athena from his head. Painted amphora, Musée du Louvre, Paris, 550–525 BCE.

---

169   Hesiod, *Theogony*: 925–926.

The story of pregnant Metis literally disappearing from sight and leaving the birth of her child to her husband is reminiscent of the creation myth in which the mother of all humans, Eve, appeared from Adam's body. Zeus was a god and Adam a human, but in both myths childbirth was undertaken by a male character.

Some stories play with this role change or make jokes about it. For example, the Hittite god Kumarbi falls pregnant when he inadvertently swallows a drop of an opponent's sperm while hitting him hard in the belly. The previously mentioned Japanese god Susanoo and his sister Amaterasu compete in producing new gods by exchanging objects and shattering his sabre and her jewels. Divine offspring pops out of their mouths – she produces three girls and he, five boys. She claims the boys and leaves the girls to him, because the boys were produced with her jewels and the girls with Susanoo's sabre.[170]

Men's armpits sometimes serve as an alternative womb, or the hollow of the knee, as in the case of the Yami in Taiwan, where one first man was created from a stone and another from a bamboo stalk.

> [They] had very long penises attached to their knee joints. Their knee joints swelled up and itched, and after a while they started to give birth. A boy burst out of the son of bamboo's right knee and a girl out of his left knee. A boy burst out of the son of stone's right knee and a girl out of his left knee. These children grew up and married each other.[171]

---

170   Hesiod in Baring and Cashford: 333ff; Pierre Lévêque: 31ff.
171   Arundel Del Rei, *Creation Myths of the Formosan Natives*. Tokyo: The Hokuseido Press, 1951 pp. 39–41. The Yami are Indonesian-related people. See also Baumann, pp. 221–224.

Inuit stories opt for a shamanic solution. After a global disaster that destroyed everything and everyone, two grown male shamans rise up from two mounds of earth. They live together and soon one of them becomes pregnant. The non-pregnant man sings a magic power song for his pregnant partner:

> A human being here A penis here.
> May its opening be wide And roomy.
> Opening, opening, opening![172]

The male anatomy got in the way of childbirth, and a change of sex was unavoidable. Hence the pregnant man's penis had to split wide open and transform into a gateway of life before he could give birth.

Those without birth-giving capacity nonetheless monopolised reproduction in societies where they were in charge. The emotions and tensions evoked by the womb are not only reflected in creation myths and religious views, but also in a global wealth of proverbs. Container metaphors are rife: pots, vases, bags, gourds, rice pans and many other objects are provided with lids and locks to protect the womb and shield it against dangers from outside.

Myths confirmed the respective roles of men and women in the process of childbirth, while supporting proverbs sustained the prevailing morality with powerful images drawn from uncertainty about the desirable answer to two crucial questions, the first regarding whose child was in the womb. Many proverbs set out that a woman should mate only with her own husband:

> Two male hippopotamuses cannot live in one pool.
> (Mandinka, Mali)

---

172 Iglulik Inuit, Canada. Knud Rasmussen, *The Netsiluk Eskimos,* 1931 p. 209.

There can only be one tiger in each cave. (Spanish, El Salvador)

Two male bears don't hibernate in one den. (Yakutsk, Russia)

You don't cook two large bones in the same pot. (Ovambo)

The eye of the needle can't hold two threads. (Arabic)

The chosen metaphors for male and female anatomy conjure the danger of female uncontrollability and insist that a monogamous relationship is a must for women. Cheating men and male desire are met with greater understanding in sayings such as, 'A thief cannot be blamed if he finds the gate open' (Colombia), or justified by arguing that his nature cannot be helped, especially in stressful times: 'In stormy weather every hole seems like a harbour,' according to wisdom from Mexico. 'Women and money tempt even Brahma the creator,' goes a Telugu saying from India. How could a man resist, if even the gods can't? The point that civilisation cannot function without self-control seems to be lacking in such arguments.[173]

The second crucial question correlates with the first – how much do male and female elements contribute to the new life budding in the womb? As this question does not have a simple answer, proverbs rarely go into the matter. It is mostly philosophers and scholars who have tried to crack the case.

Throughout history secular power and religious ideas have

---

173   See 'Messages of Metaphors', Chapter 5 of *Never Marry a Woman with Big Feet* (Yale, 2004).

bent science to their interests via subjective appreciations of physical characteristics, with blood and sperm the most striking ingredients: male fluids were clearly rated higher than female ones. In a Jewish story, undoubtedly influenced by Aristotle, God commands the soul to enter the sperm before conception takes place. The soul does not wish to descend into that 'impure' sperm, but God forces it there. Cloaked in the male reproductive cell, the soul – the superior (because: life-bringing) element – arrives in the womb where the new human being will take shape.[174]

According to Islam, only God has the power to create life, although men and women both contribute to its emergence. However, medieval Muslim theologians and doctors were inclined to present the mother as the passive partner in which the privileged male seed is planted. The Persian Muslim scholar Ibn Sina (980–1037), known as Avicenna in the West, compares male and female genitals and concludes that one set is 'complete and extends outward, while the other is incomplete and held back on the inside, as if it were an inverted male organ.'[175] Regardless, in the Quran both parents generate semen that fuses in the womb to create life. This vision is drawn from another Greek role model, Hippocrates. This two-sperm model goes against Aristotle's idea that it is men who deliver the breath of life or 'soul' to the womb. Muslim scholars from the Middle Ages preferred the version in which women's contribution to the process is diminished, whereas men's role is emphasised in intriguing ways:

Men's knowledge and expertise of the maternal body take precedence over women's experience, and, to some extent, God's omniscience. In contrast to the Quran,

---

174 Ginsberg, *The Legends of the Jews*, Vol. I: 56–57; Steenbrink p. 44.
175 Quoted in Kueny: 51; see Laqueur 1990 for similar ideas among Western scholars.

> medical writings insert themselves between God and
> the womb in order to ensure an intimate and mysterious
> partnership previously inaccessible to them.[176]

They also extensively discussed the puzzling issue as to why a child takes after one parent more than the other. Due to paternal insecurities, they were inclined to conclude that the father determines the genetic features of the child. Do phenotypic similarities then prove that a woman has not committed adultery? And if the child resembles neither of the parents, does it follow that she has been unfaithful? This problematic and distrustful reasoning also goes against the Quranic requirement that four witnesses are required to prove infidelity.

Could it be that the child would resemble the parent who was first to orgasm? To have children resemble their father, some argued, the man had to come before the woman, and with more powerful orgasms.[177] But then, why would one sperm cell be more powerful than another? It was all quite confusing. One thing, however, was agreed: 'powerful' sperm produced a son who looks like his father, and considerably increased a man's status, while a daughter diminished the father's masculinity.

Following the same line of thought, children who took after their mother (or neither parent) had to be the outcome of weak male semen unable to dominate the female contribution. To avoid such an unwanted interpretation, Islamic medical scholars preferred the hierarchical view in which the male contribution was superior, while the female body was a passive and dependent container controlled and dominated by men who embody 'the deity's elusive, ineffable efforts to produce life', with children who

---

176   Kueny p. 73.
177   *Ibid.*

resemble their fathers (instead of their mother or someone else) equated with the life that God commands:

> In order to appease paternal anxieties, male physicians see the need to de-emphasise the reproductive role of the mother, who becomes a passive recipient of prevailing male seed that must engender a child who resembles the father who sired it [...]. Such views contradict the Quran where God displays total control over the womb and its contents, or invites women to participate along with him in the production of life. In the context of the revelation, children can look like mothers, fathers, grandfathers, or no one at all. In the everyday world, however, a man must work to establish the dominant connection with his child, even if it means suppressing a woman's reproductive capacity, accusing her of adultery, or rejecting his own progeny on the basis of this similarity.[178]

In the Quran only God has unlimited power over the womb and its contents, but in earthly discussions on heredity, the man is put forward as a close second. The realisation that men could not produce offspring themselves led to interpretations reducing the uterus to a passive repository for the life-bringing sperm of men. In all three monotheistic religions, one finds theological statements plainly ignoring Eve or her contribution to the process, while eagerly confirming that all humans originate from Adam's loins (meaning: his sperm) or that his spine contained 'the great reservoir of the human race'.[179] The one who was created first

---

178 Kueny, 2013:52ff. For a wealth of information on medieval Islamic ideas, see 'Mapping the Maternal Body', Chapter 2 of *Conceiving Identities*.

179 See also Robert McElvaine, *Eve's Seed*, 2001.

assumes power over the one created later. Jewish, Christian and Islamic theologians continued to repeat this adage on the basis of a common interpretation of a story in which Eve originated from one of Adam's ribs or directly from Adam's body.

Not only in Adam and Eve stories, but also elsewhere, the desired hierarchical make-up of society was confirmed in a number of ways. The female body was reduced to a carrier of the mini-human, which the man implanted into her ready-made. Without the seed, no pregnancy. In extreme cases an animal vessel could even take over the function of the womb. In an Indian story the first man is extremely lonely after the first woman passes away. The only things he has are his cow and a thin blanket. One night he loses his seed in a dream and the next morning, he spreads out his blanket to dry on the roof. The cow pulls the blanket from the roof, eats it and becomes pregnant. She then gives birth to a boy and a girl who become the first Gadaba ancestors.[180]

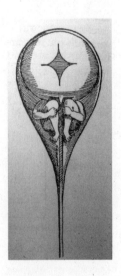 

Drawings of spermatozoa with a little human inside.
Left: Nicolaas Hartsoeker (1656–1725).
Right: Dalempatius (1670–1741).

---

180   Elwin, 1949 p. 35.

Influenced by ancestral stories and common societal values, science also held onto certain fixed ideas. Up until the seventeenth century, respected Western scholars clung to the Aristotelian view that it is the man who deposits human life into the womb – or the complete unborn child. Into the eighteenth century, various scientists continued to claim that under the microscope they had seen extremely small humans in the crawling sperm, complete with arms, legs and heads.[181] There are even drawings to 'prove' it.

The Dutch scientist Antoni van Leeuwenhoek (1632–1723) put his own sperm under a microscope and saw it move. His Delft colleague Reinier de Graaf (1641–73) carefully studied an ectopic pregnancy and noted the existence of *bollekes* ('little balls') in the female reproductive organs, leading his successors to the discovery of human egg cells. Finally, it became undeniable that both male and female reproductive cells contribute to conception and pregnancy. But still, nervous scholarly discussion was provoked as to whether a sperm cell ultimately contributed more to the emerging embryo than the female egg.

In her two-volume work *Masculin/Féminin,* anthropologist Françoise Héritier investigates the origin of the difference in appreciation of men and women. She acknowledges great differences between cultures, but also notes that everywhere power was based – and often still is – on 'the managing of reproduction, and therefore of female fertility and, in particular, of the female capacity to bear sons for men unable to do that themselves.'[182] Throughout history this unfathomable need for predominance and control has prevented interested parties from doing unprejudiced and unbiased research.

---

181   Needham: 183ff.
182   Françoise Héritier, *Masculin/Féminin II: Dissoudre la Hiérarchie,* 2002 p. 288.

Courtship and its consequences

In most creation myths there is a lack of interest in the pleasure
of sex, the dominant message being the need for reproduction.
This message has often been confirmed in proverbs: 'Women
and goats, choose them for their breed' (Spanish, Latin America)
or 'If you are impatient to have a child, you marry a pregnant
woman' (Fulfulde, West Africa).

Playing with one's own body may contribute to personal
pleasure, but not to the production of offspring – an unacceptable
outcome in a context where procreation is the main purpose of
life. God descends to the earth and punishes Adam and Eve by
depriving them of His love. From now on Adam and Eve must
earn one another's love by the sweat of their labour.[183]

The first people had to multiply and become many, as stated in
the Book of Genesis – understandable when your starting point
is an almost empty world. Sometimes, myths include references
to sexual appeal between people. A story of the Pima (or Akimel
O'odham) people of Mexico and Arizona tells how the magician
who made the world shaped two humans who 'were rather like
himself and identical with each other in every part.' Suddenly, he
realised that they had no genitals and would therefore be unable
to reproduce. He corrected his mistake:

> So he pulled a little between the legs of one image,
> saying: 'Ah, that's much better.' With his fingernail he
> made a crack in the other image. He put some pleasant
> feeling in them somewhere. 'Ah, now it's good. Now
> they'll be able to do all the necessary things.'[184]

183   *Ibid.* p. 125.
184   Richard Erdoes and Alfonso Ortiz, *American Indian Myths and Legends* (Pantheon,
      1984) p. 46 (on the basis of fragments from the 1880s).

With or without pleasure, the consequences of sex tend to turn out differently for women than for men. 'A woman hides the penis, she won't hide her swelling belly,' goes a Mamprusi observation from Burkina Faso. Myths usually don't go into the different outcomes for the sexes, but proverbs all over the world warn girls in colourful metaphors. A man may deny his involvement, but women can hide their pregnancies no better than they can conceal their love, a cough, a hunchback or riding a camel. Here are a few more:

The cow receives the bull in secret but gives birth in public. (Kurdish)

The tongue shows what it has eaten. (Lunda)

A fire and a girl's pregnancy cannot be kept secret. (Rwanda)

Love, pregnancy and going up a mountain cannot be hidden. (Arabic, Egypt)

Production within the human womb is relatively limited. In Uganda, women are sometimes compared to a field where now and then you harvest just one or two potatoes. More common is the metaphor of a jar, bowl or bag filled by the rightful owner and emptied at specific times. But then, who is the owner, and whose are the children after birth? 'A girl is like a peanut seed, she increases the clan,' according to the Congolese Woyo tradition. She is invaluable for the production of future generations and her children belong to the whole community. That idea is losing its value in times of growing individualism.

In Dar es Salaam, I was listening to a discussion between

African colleagues about who ought to own the children after a divorce. One of the men said, 'They will go to the man, of course, because he is on top when they are being made.' Everyone laughed, but when I asked him if he was serious, he said, 'Yes, in my tradition the children always go to the man.'

Obligatory female virginity remains an inexorable requirement for marriage and motherhood in many societies. The trick was to convince the woman that female chastity equated to good motherhood, to make her believe that the status of her offspring depended on her 'virtue', as Sarah Blaffer Hrdy explains in *Mother Nature*.

That message is emphasised in the universal metaphor of hens and cockerels. Desired female traits are projected onto the hen, and supposedly common male traits onto the cockerel. Cockerels who cheat on their hens are met with sympathy for their natural promiscuity. Old or young, it is argued, they are all the same – though he may refuse to eat with a hen who is laying another cockerel's egg. Hens should only mate with their own cockerel, content with their position as one of his many partners, otherwise her male partner is 'cuckolded'.

As surviving without a cockerel is out of the question, a sensible hen avoids quarrelling and adopts an attitude of submissiveness. Her motherly love is expressed in metaphors of warm feathers and wings for all her chicks. Cockerels should do the crowing and hens stay silent, because the reverse would cause the house to 'collapse' (Japanese) and the family to be 'doomed' (Chinese). What is wisdom? 'The hen knows when it is morning, but she looks at the mouth of the cockerel,' as an Ashanti proverb puts it. In other words, let him carry the conversation while she looks after their brood. God help the pitiful coop where the hens are crowing while the cockerel is mothering the chicks!

Dangerous childbirth and safe contraception

Pregnancy and delivery have always been a significant cause of
death for women and babies. Today childbirth remains a risky
activity and is the cause of death for hundreds of thousands of
women globally. Thousands of years ago, the Sumerians voiced
concerns about the precarious fate of a woman frequently in labour:
'A mother who gave birth to eight sons, lies down in weakness.'
No wonder such a productive woman is scared of another
pregnancy. The Haya in Tanzania also voice disapproval at the
eighth birth: 'The woman who said, "How well and easily I give
birth," died with the birth of her ninth child.' Indeed, 'Pregnant
women have one foot in the grave,' according to a German
saying; a Vietnamese warning similarly observes: 'A pregnant
woman stands at the brink of the graveyard;' and Papiamentu-
speaking people of the West Indies used to worry that 'The last
child kills its mother.' Even though most women and men want
children, their wish is not limitless, and it's questionable whether
the following sayings are positive:

Two can make ten. (Mongolian)

Under bad stars a woman gives birth to two babies a
year. (Pashto, Afghanistan)

Every year a child and in nine years, twelve. (Bulgarian).

Nonetheless, there are plenty of boasts about men who produce
many offspring. And men are not at risk at the moment they
become fathers. On the contrary, 'He who fathers offspring, never
dies,' is a triumphant statement in Arabic. A unique example
in the field of male immortality was Moroccan sultan Moulay

Roman terracotta votive of a pregnant woman, Suffolk, England. Wellcome Collection, London. *c.* 100 BCE–200 CE.

Ismail Ibn Sharif (1646–1727), who fathered forty sons in a period of three months, and an impressive total of 888 children via his many wives and concubines. After his death, a beautiful mausoleum was built in his honour in Meknes. But perhaps the absolute fathering champion was the Mongolian ruler Genghis Khan, who is said to have sired more than a thousand children. Whichever of them was the biggest daddy, one thing is absolutely certain: the matter of producing heirs only rarely causes a man's death – and then it's more likely at conception than at birth.

Today, we have access to birth control, but this doesn't mean that male control of female sexuality is no longer on the agenda. Slightly embarrassed, a Turkish restaurant owner in London shared with me his father's favourite saying: 'A stick on the back and a child in the womb' – while beseeching me to believe that he did not share his father's opinion at all.

He went on to explain that in the past, in his country of birth, men believed this was the only way to control women. The men supporting that statement must have been really afraid of female power. And of course, prominent Catholic clergy still ban contraception, obediently following Pope Paul VI, in his 1968 encyclical, Humanae Vitae, about marital love: 'Finally, this love is fecund. It is not confined wholly to the loving interchange of husband and wife; it also contrives to go beyond this to bring new life into being. Marriage and conjugal love are by their nature ordained toward the procreation and education of children.'[185]

---

185   Pope Paul VI, Humanae Vitae, The Holy See, July 25 1968. Accessed via Vatican.va.

Statuette of a nourishing mother, Phemba fertility cult, Kingdom of Kongo (Mayombe, DR Congo), Wellcome Collection, London. *c.* 1880.

CHAPTER SEVEN

THE MAGIC OF THE NOURISHING NIPPLE

Whatever you sucked from the tit, will be spilt over your grave.
(Spanish, Bolivia)

THE MILK OF Mother Goddesses and the Virgin Mary is widely perceived as possessing miraculous powers. But in various cultures, the breast milk of ordinary women is also believed to have magical effects. The belief that 'Mothers' milk is holy,' as a Mongolian proverb has it, probably goes too far, but ideas of breastfeeding passing on good (and bad) qualities is widespread.

From the nipple to the grave

In ancient Rome, slave women were used as nurses, but there were also professional wet-nurses for rent at a spot called *Columna Lactaria* (Milk Pillar or Column). These women were proud of their profession and able to negotiate a good salary. Greek nurses were in especially high demand among Roman civilians, in the belief that the baby would suck up the language of the nurse via their milk so that in addition to Latin, the child would speak fluent Greek.

The seventeenth-century Dutch poet Jacob Cats thought that a child who suckled a stranger's milk would acquire a dubious character; a true mother would never trust someone else to do her maternal duty:

> Employ O young wife, your precious gifts
> There is nothing an upright man would rather see
> Than his dear wife bid the child to the teat
> This bosom that you carry, so swollen up with life
> So finely wrought, as if it were ivory orbs.[186]

Cats was far from alone in the opinion that breast milk affected a child's psyche. In nineteenth-century France, there was even a bill preventing mothers of bad moral reputation from nursing their own babies. Among Muslims there is a traditional fear of Jewish, Christian or worse, *kafir* milk, the milk of an unbeliever, that would sway the baby's faith. When an Islamic mother is unable to breastfeed her own baby, the wet-nurse must meet other requirements too. The Prophet Muhammad instructed Muslims to protect their children against drinking the milk of 'adulteresses and madwomen'.[187]

Milk has to be halal, is the reasoning, and no modern milk bank can fully guarantee that milk is of Islamic origin. In Turkey, using donor milk is relatively common and thought to considerably lower the death rate of children in rural areas, but the question

---

186 Jacob Cats, *Moeder, Houwelijck*, (Simon Schama's translation) quoted in Hufton, *The Prospect Before Her* (Vintage, 1996) p. 200.

187 Ulfat Shaikh and Omar Ahmed, 'Islam and Infant Feeding' in *Breastfeeding Medicine* Autumn;1(3):164–167. (2006) p. 164.

of whether a child that has been nursed by an atheist is doomed to grow up to be an unbeliever is still a matter of debate between Islamic scholars and medical doctors.

Romulus, Remus and the she-wolf. Bronze, Capitoline Museums, Rome. Twelfth century.

At the breast of an animal, or an animal at the breast

The Swedish scientist Carl Linnaeus's view was that a child breastfed by a lioness would imbibe great courage. It is unclear as to whether this observation was based on scientific research. Of all the stories about human babies breastfed by a wild animal, that of Romulus and Remus is one of the best known. In Roman culture Diva Rumina was the patron goddess of nursing human and animal mothers. Her temple was located near the fig tree under which, according to the story, the two boys had been nursed. The founders of Rome had been abandoned by their mother after a pregnancy due to rape, and the two babies were close to dying of hunger when a she-wolf took care of them.

The Jewish Talmud allowed babies to be fed by a female animal if the wellbeing of the child depended on it. The Islamic tradition discouraged the feeding of babies with animal milk out of fear that the child would gain animal characteristics. In Christian circles the topic was much less discussed. In a late nineteenth-century French drawing, two women each hold a drinking baby under the belly of a female donkey, while a woman with a third baby is waiting her turn. Thanks to the milk of she-donkeys a charitable orphanage kept the abandoned babies alive.[188]

In the eighteenth and nineteenth centuries goats became more and more popular as wet-nurses. In 1816 a German writer even published a book with the title *The Goat as the Best and Most Agreeable Wet-Nurse*. Not only was she a lot cheaper than a hired wet-nurse, but also a lot safer during times of syphilis and other deadly diseases.

There are also instances where women would lovingly breastfeed baby animals: fawns, monkeys, puppies or piglets, either to help the animal survive (for religious or commercial reasons) or for pure affection. In Central America, Western travellers came across women of different cultures breastfeeding various kinds of young animals such as squirrels, possums, wild cats and boars.[189] Among some people in Papua New Guinea it is not uncommon to put your own baby on one breast and a piglet on the other. 'The pig is our heart,' is the explanation.

188   Osborn, M.S. 'The Rent Breasts: A Brief History of Wet-nursing' in *Midwife, Health Visitor & Community Nurse*, 1979; 15(8): 302–306; Samuel X. Radbill, 'The Role of Animals in Infant Feeding' in Wayland D. Hand, *American Folk Medicine: A Symposium* (University of California Press, 1976).

189   Karin Brulliard, 'Why Goats Used to Breastfeed Human Babies', *Washington Post*, 25 February 2016.

Putting a small animal on the breast also served to harden the nipples of inexperienced mothers or relieve engorged breasts, but Westerners seem to have forgotten these old customs and remedies. Instead, the very idea provokes shocked reactions, as recently happened in Ireland, where emotions ran high at a picture on a calendar of a famous model breastfeeding a little dog. In another example in the United States, people were shocked by the cover of the album *Boys for Pele*, depicting the singer Tori Amos breastfeeding a piglet. Such reactions reflect a need for concrete boundaries between humans and animals, or between culture and nature.

Orphan babies being nursed by she-donkeys. French engraving, 1895.

Supplementary breasts

During the European Renaissance wealthy women refused to breastfeed their own children. 'In a century where the erotic potential of the breast began to obscure its maternal function, many ladies were simply not willing to devote themselves fully to their babies at the expense of their relations with their husbands, not to mention their lovers,' writes Marilyn Yalom, and so they happily hired wet-nurses. But they were also put under serious pressure:

> The practice of sending babies away to rural wet-nurses was roundly condemned by medical doctors, humanists, priests, preachers and other moralists throughout Europe. A body of literature sprang up during the Renaissance declaring that it was a mother's duty to breastfeed and that the use of a wet-nurse was a risky substitute for the biological mother. […] Some moral arbiters went so far as to call the refusal to breastfeed one's own child a sin, especially in countries like Germany and England, where Protestant reformers were calling for a more stringent morality.[190]

Nonetheless, out of the fear of sagging breasts, many women were sending their babies to the countryside for as long as twenty-four months. In upper-class families a wet-nurse came to live in the home. François Clouet's famous painting *La Dame au Bain* (1571) reflects not only the class differences of his time, but also the contrast between erotic and nursing breasts. In the foreground, between draped red curtains, stands a chestnut bathtub in which an unknown lady sits – possibly a young Mary Queen of Scots. She wears a diadem in her hair and a pearl on her forehead, and she has striking, relatively small, bare breasts, which have managed to maintain their youthful shape due to the hired wet-nurse behind her. The wet-nurse has a swaddled baby at her ample breast, while in the background a servant girl warms water for the lady's bath.

---

190   Yalom pp. 70–71.

Goat as a nursing mother. Cuba, 1903.

The breasts of the woman in the bath are meant to please, those of the wet-nurse to work for her daily bread.

Being a wet-nurse was usually a labour of love, but with rising demand the value of the job went up, allowing many women to earn a good living by their breast milk. The wealthier the infant's parents, the more influential the wet-nurse:

> Those who found themselves at the very highest levels, such as the wet-nurses attached to the family of the pharaoh, were the equivalent of the great court ladies presiding over significant networks of power. The wet-nurses to the queens of France were entitled to any number of perks, including the name 'Madame Poitrine' (Mrs Breast), which was worn like a badge of honour in certain French families long after the monarchy had disappeared.[191]

---

191   Yalom p. 160.

Priest deflowering a bride. The groom is in the hallway waiting his turn. Persian manuscript of Al-Qazwini, 1203–1283.

Gabrielle Palmer, author of *The Politics of Breastfeeding* (2009), discovered that being a wet-nurse in seventeenth- and eighteenth-century England was a great job that could provide a woman with a higher salary than her husband. As a royal wet-nurse one was honoured 'for life'. In England, legendary wet-nurse Judith Waterford was able in her prime to effortlessly produce almost two litres [four pints] of milk a day, and on her eighty-first birthday in 1831 was still producing breast milk.[192]

The profession of wet-nurse dates back to ancient times. In Mesopotamia a wet-nurse was hired for two to three years and could be paid in kind in barley, oil, wool or even silver. An old Sumerian saying even proclaims that wet-nurses determined the fate of kings in the women's quarters. This may seem exaggerated, but it does show that these women had huge responsibilities. If

---

192   Viv Groskop: 'Not Your Mother's Milk', *Guardian Health*, 5 January 2007.

a baby died while in the care of a wet-nurse, it was immediately assumed that she had taken on a second baby without the consent of the parents. Such a serious accusation had to be proved, but in the case of Hammurabi's law (*c.* 1780 BCE) the punishment was harsh: 'cut off the breasts'.[193]

A similar wet-nurse tradition existed in China. The last Chinese emperor Pu Yi (1906–67) felt extremely unhappy when he was suddenly ceremonially crowned while still a child. His wet-nurse Wen-Chao Wang was the only one who could comfort him. He developed a close connection with her and she probably breastfed him till his teenage years. During the Cultural Revolution Mao abolished this 'decadence', but after a long political prohibition the old custom returned to Chinese society. No doubt the worldwide-reported bottle-milk scandal – whereby some manufacturers of infant formula in China adulterated the powder with the chemical melamine – contributed to a new legion of highly paid wet-nurses. This serious food safety incident in China dated back to 2007, but was made public in September 2008 when it was reported that, as result of the contaminated milk, 'Kidney and urinary tract effects, including kidney stones, affected about 300,000 Chinese infants and young children, with six reported deaths.'[194]

Once again, wealthy Chinese families went in search of healthy pregnant village women who, right after delivering their own baby, were willing to breastfeed the baby of a well-off city woman. Their own children stay behind with the grandparents in the village, who try to find a cheap local wet-nurse for the remaining newborn. This sacrifice is made up for by the lucrative salaries super-rich families are willing to pay.

193   Marten Stol, *Women in the Ancient Near East* (De Gruyte, 2016).
194   'Food Safety incidents in China', Wikipedia, Wikimedia Foundation. Last edited 27 October 2023.

The demand for wet-nurses is also rising among Hollywood celebrities, many of whom are either unwilling to breastfeed or unable to because of breast implants. However, a license is needed, because outsourced breastfeeding can be construed as child abuse. There was a case in Oklahoma in 2003 where a woman breastfed someone else's baby without consent and faced a fine of five hundred dollars and a jail sentence of up to a year for having bad morals.[195]

Charitable nursing

There's no end of stories about selfless nursing nipples that give the woman who own them extra lustre. The Prophet Muhammad had several successive wet-nurses, according to tradition. The first was Halima who, during a disastrous drought and driven by need, went with other women to Mecca, searching for a wet-nurse job even though she could hardly feed her own child. When the women reached Mecca, they were, one after the other, offered the Prophet as an infant to be nursed. They all declined, because Muhammad's father Abdullah had died six months prior to the Prophet's birth, and to raise an orphan would only result in more hardship. Not finding any other baby to suckle, Halima went back and decided to take him. As soon as she put him on her breast, 'the milk started flowing miraculously'. She nursed the Prophet on one breast and her own son on the other, and both babies were fully satisfied. Moreover, her female camel, who on the road hadn't given a single drop of milk, suddenly had a full udder again. For sure, Halima had 'a blessed soul' at her breast.[196]

195   Groskop, *ibid*.
196   Kueny, Chapter 4 and Islam Web, 'Wet-nurses of Prophet Muhammad – II', 5
       January 2012.

The breastfeeding of a needy relative was considered an act of the highest charity in many traditions globally.[197] The all-sacrificing love of daughters for parents or in-laws is an important theme in many breastfeeding stories. The exemplary daughter-in-law nursing her illustrious mother-in-law has been portrayed as an example of pure harmony in China – an ideal that goes against widespread proverbial wisdom about the relationship of a young wife and her mother-in-law.

François Clouet, La Dame au bain. Two types of breasts, 1571.

In Rome, the story of Cimon and Pero was presented as an exemplary act of piety and honour. Cimon is an old man, imprisoned and condemned to starvation. Visitors are allowed, but bringing food is forbidden. To keep him alive, his daughter Pero visits and breastfeeds her father every day. When he is still

---

197 The Epoch Times, 'Filial Piety Touches Heaven: stories of virtuous daughters-in-law'. With thanks to colleague and sinologist Wilt Idema for clarifying information about the image.

alive after a month, a jailer spies on them and catches them in the act. The judges to whom he reports are so moved by this great parental love, that the daughter is not punished for her offence and the old man is released.

The ambience shifts when the parent in need is of the other sex. In the Western world, this story became a valid theme in the arts, partly due to the tension between charity and the erotic, incestuous implications of a father drinking from his daughter's youthful breast. There is less room for erotic associations when the artist zooms in on the imminent death of a declining man with ageing features and untidy grey hair, or on the rusty irons that confine him to his cheerless cell (Peter Paul Rubens: *Roman Charity*, c. 1612.

Exemplary Chinese daughter-in-law suckles her old mother-in-law. Ivory, date unknown.

In some paintings the daughter's sleeping baby lies on the cell floor (Rubens) or she feeds her father from outside, through the bars that separate them, as in Caravaggio's *The Seven Works of Mercy* (1607). The Turkish artist Ferhad Özgür was also inspired by this dramatic situation to make a short film. It impressed many viewers, but not those (presumably unfamiliar with the ancient story) who condemned it as 'sick porn'.[198]

Peter Paul Rubens, *Roman Charity*, daughter breastfeeding her father in the prison, 1612.

---

198 Accessed via https://www.youtube.com/watch?v=c33499mGtAk, unfortunately no longer available due to a copyright claim.

Cornelis Corneliszoon van Haarlem, *The Miracle of Haarlem*, 1591.

The history of a renowned painting in the Frans Hals Museum in Haarlem reflects how people's views change when they have more information about a story or image's cultural background. The artwork, painted in 1591 by Cornelis Cornelisz of Haarlem, entitled *A Monk and a Nun*, was also recorded in museum records as *The Miracle of Haarlem*.

According to legend a nun was accused of having become pregnant. To verify this a monk had to squeeze her breast and if it produced milk, she was guilty. But instead of milk she produced wine – the reason for the wine glass on the table. Instead of proving the nun's guilt the miracle was witness to her faith. Yet the legend may not have been the real subject of the painting. Pictures of amorous monks and nuns were a popular genre in the late sixteenth century. This may in fact be a satire on the immorality of the cloisters and the Catholic Church.[199]

Perhaps the artist's intentions were playfully ambiguous.

---

199 See Frans Hals Museum, 'A Monk and a Nun', commentary by Cornelisz van Haarlem on a painting of the same name.

Artemis of Ephesus, the 'Great Mother Goddess'. Roman copy, marble and bronze, Capitoline Museums, Rome, second century BCE.

CHAPTER EIGHT

MAMMALIA

To the river that took him, the old man screamed:
'Mamma!'
(Adyghe)

LINNAEUS DERIVED HIS classification of humans and other lactating animals as *mammalia* from the Latin word *mamma* meaning not only 'breast', but also 'mother' or 'nurse'. The intimate relationship between mother and child starts at the breast, and words connecting breast and milk exist in various languages. The Chinese word for milk is *ru*, and the breast is referred to as *rǔfáng*, literally meaning 'milk house'. In the Amerindian language, Quechua, the word for the motherly breast, *ñuñu*, comes together with the verb 'to drink breast milk'. In Africa too the words for breast and milk often coincide, for example, in Swahili *ziwa* means 'breast' and *maziwa* 'milk'. The same holds for the Austronesian languages in the South Sea, Madagascar and most islands of Southeast Asia: two ancient forms (*susu* and *nunuh*) come up in one form or another. Both mean 'breast', and often also have the meaning of milk, mother and feeding. In many languages the word mother or mama means literally 'the woman who gave me breast milk'.[200] There are no erotic connotations in any of those meanings.

Mamma

Lactation developed in the mid- to late-Triassic period about 200 million years ago as a form of nutrition and protection against infections. Before family planning, the breasts of our foremothers produced milk for about half the time between puberty and menopause. All in all, a woman spent ten years of her life nursing, and during her fertile life produced about 1,350 litres of milk.[201]

In many cultures there was a taboo on having sex with women nursing a child. Women fed their babies for at least a year or two; those who didn't were pregnant again within a few months. Breastfeeding is no safe means of birth control, but when the baby sucks on the breast, hormones are released (prolactin and oxytocin) that reduce the growth of the egg cell and obstruct the build-up of the womb lining. Gradually the child will drink less often or at greater intervals, and the chance of conception increases.

Even in medical circles, breast milk was understood to be 'adapted blood'. Since women did not menstruate during their pregnancies, it was believed that women transformed blood into food for their babies. The process of nursing mothers turning blood into milk would be endangered by having sex: it would disrupt the flow of milk, and might even kill the newly formed foetus. Thanks to that common misunderstanding, women were

---

200 With thanks to culture and language specialists: Sander Adelaar (Melbourne); Willem Adelaar (Leiden); Willem van der Molen (Jakarta); Aldin Mutembei (Dar es Salaam) and Kristofer Schipper (Fuzhou).

201 Geoffrey Miller, *The Mating Mind*, (Vintage Books, 2001) pp. 242–243.

granted a brief period of relief with a child or two on the breast before the next pregnancy announced itself.[202]

Unlike humans, other mammals' nipples hang beneath the body and out of sight: they only have a nursing function and become flat again after the nursing period. Since our ancestors started walking upright, male genitals and female breasts came into direct view. It remains guesswork as to what time in human evolution female breasts gained their full shape, even when not graced with milk. But for *Homo erectus*, breasts became a sign of health and fertility and a selection criterion for partner choice.

Sitting Mother Goddess breastfeeding two children. Valkhof Museum, Nijmegen. Second century CE.

---

202 Thomas Laqueur, *Making Sex: Body and Gender from the Greeks to Freud*, 1990 p. 36; Yalom p. 70.

Supernumerary breasts

One of the Seven Wonders of the Ancient World, the sanctuary of the Greek goddess Artemis, was located in Ephesus in present-day Turkey. Due to the many round bulges protruding from the front of various Artemis statues, the Greeks gave her the nickname 'many-breasted one'. Supplementary breasts also occur in humans. In the medical world the phenomenon is called polymastia. But during puberty usually only two mammary glands develop into breasts:

> If we were rats or pigs, our twin milk strips would develop into a total of eight teats, to meet the demands of large litters. Mammals such as elephants, cows, goats and primates, which give birth to only one or two offspring at a time, require only two mammary glands, and so the bulk of the milk strip regresses during fetal development.[203]

Extra mammary glands usually don't develop into fully formed breasts, but after birth-giving they may produce milk. In 1886, a case was reported in Europe of a twenty-three-year-old woman with six additional breasts. After her first delivery nothing special happened, but after her second, all eight started leaking milk.

All kinds of stories have been told about polymastia. Women with more than two breasts were seen as monsters and put on show. Medical doctor and philosopher Fortunio Liceti wrote a book about this phenomenon, published and popularised in Amsterdam in 1665, eight years after his death. Anne Boleyn, the unhappy wife of Henry VIII, who was persecuted as an

---

203   Nathalie Angier, *Woman: An Intimate Geography*, 1999 pp. 141–142.

Illustration from the 1665 edition of Fortunio Liceti's *De Monstris*. Leiden University Libraries.

adulteress, was said to have a third breast, a story that undoubtedly contributed to her discredit. Women with more than two nipples risked being accused of witchcraft in earlier centuries:

> Witch-hunters often had their suspects stripped and publicly examined for signs of an unsightly blemish that witches were said to receive upon making their pact with Satan. [...] Prosecutors might also search for the 'witches' teat', an extra nipple allegedly used to suckle the witch's helper animals. In both cases, it was easy for even the most minor physical imperfections to be labeled as the work of the devil himself. Moles, scars, birthmarks, sores, supernumerary nipples and tattoos could all qualify, so examiners rarely came up empty-handed.[204]

Pupazza frascatana. Musée des Civilisations de l'Europe et de la Méditerranée (MUCEM), Marseille, *c.* 1960.

---

204   *Cultural Encyclopedia of the Breast*, 2014:264ff; '7 Bizarre Witch Trial Tests' by Evan Andrews, *Sky History*, 18 March 2014.

In the town of Frascati in Italy, biscuits known as *pupazze frascatana* are baked in the shape of a woman with three breasts and are seen in every baker's window. The caption of one I found one in Marseille's MUCEM gives her name as Gina, in sweet memory of former movie star Gina Lollobrigida. Legend has it that two breasts produced milk and the third, wine. According to some the tradition goes back to ancient bacchanalia, while others believe it was a brilliant invention of wet-nurses in the Renaissance: a fake breast filled with wine would soothe children into sleep in no time.

Milk ties as a ban on sex

Modern-day developments burden traditional believers with dilemmas and bring forth juridical advice from religious authorities or spiritual leaders that is not always easy to obey in practice.

On the basis of the Islamic prohibition of sexual relations between a man and the woman who once nursed him, in 2007 an Islamic scholar issued a *fatwa* that decreed breastfeeding to be the perfect solution for the growing problem of undesirable interactions between men and women in the workplace, instructing women to breastfeed their male colleagues. After five feeds, 'milk ties' are established, preventing any sexual relations. Thus the religious ban on mixed company could be lifted without violating Islamic law. Women would even be allowed to have their hair uncovered in the presence of the men they had nursed.[205]

The initiator, Dr Izzat Atiya, a specialist on the Prophet

---

205 Sam Shamoun, 'Islam and the Nursing of Adults' in *Answering Islam: A Christian-Muslim Dialog* by M. Rafiqul-Haqq and P. Newton.

Muhammad's statements at Cairo's prestigious Al-Azhar University, based this *fatwa* on medieval interpretations of a minority point of view insisting on the strict separation of sexes. This is based on the belief that when a man and a woman meet who are not direct relatives, Satan will be the third-party present and that always means trouble. The *fatwa* caused uproar, was ridiculed in the media and was soon withdrawn by an Al-Azhar committee because it contradicted the principles of Islam and morality.[206]

Ultra-orthodox Islamic scholars continue to pressure each other and other believers to hold on to real or supposed statements by the Prophet Muhammad.[207] The extremely diverse comments on this fatwa make clear that the motherly and sexual function of breasts are easily mixed up and get in each other's way.

On Islamic websites believers often ask whether a man can drink his wife's breast milk. Is it only halal if you spit it out at once? The answers of Muslim clergy contradict each other. On the one hand, a husband is allowed to 'enjoy his wife in whatever way he wants, such as kissing, touching, looking, etc. [...] if he sucks on her nipples, this comes under the heading of the intimacy that is permissible.' According to some imams, however, it is better that a man avoids drinking his wife's breast milk, even though it has 'no effect'. To be safe, they always add that 'Allah knows everything the best.'[208]

Examples of traditional 'milk tie' relations are widespread. From Afghanistan and India to North Africa and the Balkans,

---

206 'Breastfeeding fatwa causes stir', BBC News, 22 May 2007.

207 Extensive information on the withdrawn fatwa about obligatory breastfeeding to male adults at work can be found in *Naked or Covered*: 179ff; see also Islam Question and Answer general supervisor Shaykh Muhammad Saalih al-Munajjid, 'Can Husband Drink Milk of Wife in Islam?', 25 October 1998.

208 See Islam Question and Answer general supervisor Shaykh Muhammad Saalih al-Munajjid, 'Can Husband Suck Wife's Breasts?', 3 March 2004.

breast milk, that unique nourishment, fulfils special needs.[209] The creation of such a bond can, for example, save a relationship about to break.

In Georgia, if a husband thought his wife unfaithful, he called the suspected paramour to his house, bared his wife's right breast, put salt on it, and asked the man to kiss it. The suspect had no option: if he kissed it, he would be milk-tied to the woman for life and so could not, under threat of punitive retribution, have sex with her; if he did not kiss it, he incriminated himself and faced punitive retribution. Once the deed was done, the husband would address the couple: 'Man, behold your mother. Woman, behold your son.' He could now rest assured; his wife and new milk son-in-law could meet openly without fear of raising any suspicion, for incest was out of the question.[210]

In another example, a Palestinian woman publicly pushed her breast into a male stranger's mouth with the words, 'You are my son in the Book of God, you have drunk from my breast.' The reasoning behind this ritual adoption was that a woman on the road for some time with a man not belonging to her close family was thus able to protect her respectability.[211]

Erotic lactation

The verb 'to nipple' does not seem to exist in the English, but I for one would champion it. In Dutch, it was in the dictionary until the nineteenth century, meaning 'intensely fondling a woman's breasts out of lewd passion.' *Nippelen* originates from *nijpen*, meaning 'to pinch', but nippling is doing it nicely without hurting.

209 Jeremy MacClancy, 'The Milk Tie' in *Anthropology of Food*, 2 September 2003 p. 229.
210 *Ibid.* p. 25.
211 Granqvist in MacClancy p. 23.

Joost van den Vondel, for example, used it in his play *Samson, or Holy Revenge* (1660), when referring to Samson passionately caressing Delilah.[212] Apparently this was the correct term for the affectionate sucking, petting and pinching of the nipples. The term may have disappeared, but the practice has not.

Fervent fondling, kneading and massaging stimulates milk production. A woman of sixty-five, the mother of adult children, went to see a gynaecologist in Amsterdam because milk was flowing from her breasts. She thought she had cancer, but after being questioned by the gynaecologist, the origin of this innocent phenomenon was that her husband couldn't get enough of nippling her. Due to his loving attention, lactation had spontaneously got going again. A woman doesn't even need to have been pregnant to produce milk.

Natural breastfeeding for babies may develop into a nostalgic breastfeeding relationship between adults. Where does motherly nursing end and erotic lactation begin? From research in 2005 carried out among 1,700 British men it appeared that more than 30 per cent not only enthusiastically fondled their partner, but also happily drank from the breast along with the baby. The main reason provided was 'emotional need'.[213] The research doesn't mention whether these men hadn't had enough breastfeeding as babies.

The oldest profession has been modulated to meet this emotional need among adult men, which is referred to as lactophilia or milk fetishism or, with obvious disdain, as infantilism – especially when a man wants to crawl back into the baby-on-the-breast role, and is willing to pay for being given a treat by mommy (sometimes even with a nappy on), as if to play

212   Cf. *Nieuw woordenboek der Nederlandsche taal*, 1864 pp. 12–24.

213   Lois Rogers, 'Earth Dads Give Breast Milk a Try'. *The Sunday Times*, 13 March 2005; see also 'erotic lactation' on Wikipedia.

out incestuous desires. Instances of 'lactation prostitution' can be found all over the world.[214]

In 1903, the German philosopher Carl Buttenstedt warmly recommended erotic lactation as both a natural form of birth control and a source of sexual pleasure. His book was well received, but critics also warned against the danger of pathological arousal of sexual feelings in both partners. In 1938 the book was forbidden by the Nazis as harmful.[215]

Serving breast milk to adults was once considered an act of charity towards needy elders and prisoners. In England there are mentions of breastfeeding used as medicine as early as in 1655, recommended as a treatment for adults suffering from eye diseases and tuberculosis.[216]

Over the last couple of years, the benefits of breastfeeding for adults have been rediscovered in China. On various websites the service of wet-nurses is offered for ailing adults as well as infants. Customers can choose whether they want to drink the milk directly from the breast or from a glass. Pictures of young mothers are provided for men to choose from, clearly to tempt some who are not seeking medical assistance. By taking out a subscription to Mother Nature's smoothie, customers can always return to their favourite breasts. From time to time, a group of women is arrested for online sales of their milk, as disapprovingly reported in various newspapers:

The crooks allegedly hired mothers with newborn babies to breastfeed adults and, according to the newspaper report, the women fed their babies powdered milk to

214   *Ibid.*
215   Carl Buttenstedt was the author of *Die Glücks-Ehe: die Offenbarung im Weibe, eine Naturstudie* ('The Happy Marriage').
216   *Ibid.*; Mary Prior, *Women in English Society*, 1500–1800, (Routledge, 1991) p. 6.

concentrate on selling breast milk for business. China's Ministry of Public Security coordinated with police to break up two gangs involved in the business, the report said. The police said more than 200 people from across the country paid for the breastfeeding and prostitution services advertised on websites. According to a local newspaper, there were several websites that offered to provide young mothers to breastfeed adults for a fee.[217]

Is breastfeeding a new way to show how wealthy you are in China? In Shenzhen, adults who can afford it are hiring wet-nurses for the special nutritional value of breast milk. Those with a demanding job, poor personal health and a high income can take on a wet-nurse for daily personal use – at a salary of between 12,000 and 20,000 yuan a month.[218]

A woman who had been in the business herself mentioned that there are two types of customers: those who want only the milk, the so-called clean service, and those who wanted more, referred to as the dirty service. A number of mothers only got regular customers if they were also willing to offer sexual services, according to the *Beijing News*.[219]

Most Chinese internet users reacted to the story with indignation: ethical values were being violated and women treated as consumer goods.[220] All at a time when the Chinese

217   'Chinese women gang sells own milk to men with breastfeeding fetish', *India Today*, 1 January 2015.

218   The original source for this was available at https://qz.com/103834/in-china-whealthy-adults-drink-breast-milk-while-millions-of-infants-stick-with-formula. However, the Chinese government has deleted many sources, and this web page no longer exists. In the Chinese translation of my previous book, all references to China's wet-nurses were also heavily censored.

219   'Chinese women gang sells own milk to men with breastfeeding fetish', *India Today*, 1 January 2015.

220   'Erotic Lactation,' Wikipedia, Wikimedia Foundation. Last edited 5 November 2023.

government had made every effort to promote breastfeeding among young mothers – especially since a couple of serious bottle-milk scandals led to the tragic deaths of babies.

In Tokyo the Bonyu Bar (Mother's Milk Bar) hires women for the service of its customers. Their work consists of pouring and serving a glass of breast milk for the equivalent of about fifteen euros or offering the milk directly from the breast for two or three times as much. In the latter case women are also prepared to ruffle the hair, whisper the name and offer sweet words of comfort into the ear of the customer sucking on the nipple. Most customers are between thirty and forty years old.[221]

The examples from China and Japan are not the only paid-for transactions. Men in other parts of the world also seem to like to be cuddled by a nursing mother. A Nigerian man confessed that he had once tried it out with his ex-girlfriend and it turned out to be an intimate and beneficial experience. He sought out the woman again and now pays for the service. Even though he admits the relationship looks sexually loaded, it does not mean sexual pleasure to him, but intimacy. Another man found his wife nursing their first baby so erotic that 'her breasts dripping with milk turned him on.'[222]

A long article in the Nigerian *New Telegraph Online* discussed the fundamental question: to whom do breasts belong, the husband or the baby? It collected a number of comments on fathers' envy of babies taking over and claiming the breasts they considered their property. The discussion flared up during World

---

221 The original source for this was available at https://www.atlantico.fr/antlantico-light/japon-prendrez-biern-verre-lait-maternel-1974264.html #9m3mpYQ4xxmSZqB6.99. Unfortunately it, too, has been removed. This is important information, and originally existed as part of a long article on the debate surrounding breast milk from 2016, based on a questionnaire around the issue.

222 'Nigeria: 'Adult Nursing'– Men Who Compete With Babies Over Breast Milk!', by Femi Ajasa, 18 January 2016, available on *All Africa*.

Breastfeeding Week (the first week of August) after the Lagos State Commissioner for Information had seriously advised fathers to stop competing with their babies for ownership of breasts:

> Rather than compete with the infants, men should encourage their wives to engage in exclusive breastfeeding which is vital for infants especially during their first six months. His statement, however, generated a lot of mixed reactions from men; many objecting vehemently to what he said with some even arguing that their wife's breasts are their exclusive property and not for their babies.[223]

Summarising the mainly humorous reactions, they avow that it's the man who is the rightful owner: 'I need those breasts more than the baby, because they belong to me and are part of the price that I paid dowry for.' Or: 'The baby may have leased them for a time, but they are mine!' And: 'Their perfect roundness and warmth are the reason why I suck on the breasts of my wife, whether or not she is feeding a baby.' The majority openly insist that 'breasts belong exclusively to the man' or, in the carefully considered words of one businessman:

> The man is the full custodian of the breast, but must take backstage when the baby is on the show. Both man and baby need the breast; while one needs it for nutrition and that is for a season, the other needs it for satisfaction and for keeps. [...] The baby owns the milk but I own the breast.

---

223   'Breastfeeding Wives', *New Telegraph*, August 2017.

In another newspaper, *The Nation*, the topic is dealt with from a women's perspective, and they seem to agree with the men. One example:

> My husband has the right of first refusal. My view is that the man owns the breast, not the baby. When a woman is breastfeeding, the baby can claim ownership of the breast, [But] after the breastfeeding period, the breast goes back to the husband until the woman conceives again. So, it's only during breastfeeding that a child can lay claim to the breast. If not, the husband owns the breast.[224]

The idea of a woman as the owner of her own body and body parts is entirely absent.

Breast milk remains an intriguing phenomenon in many respects. It has even been experimented with in dishes. Some websites advertise recipes for breast milk ice cream, butter, cheese and yoghurt; muffins, bread and cakes; breast milk risotto with mushrooms; breast milk lasagne and breast milk fruit shakes. Initiatives using breast milk as an ingredient for production and sale tend to have a short life. A cheese was produced by New York restaurant owner Daniel Angerer with milk from his own wife, which he served as a complimentary canapé with figs and Hungarian pepper. The restaurant was immediately given a warning by the New York City Health Department that prohibited further production and sales.[225] The same fate awaited a dessert served in a London restaurant called Baby

---

224 Precious Dikehowa: 'Should Men Stay off Wives' Breasts?', *The Nation*, 23 October 2015.

225 'Brace yourself for the Mother of All Cheeses' by Emine Saner, *The Guardian*, 9 March 2010.

Gaga Breast Milk Ice Cream. Despite having been prepared from carefully selected milk made available by mothers approved by the National Health Service as blood donors, this special ice cream was confiscated within a few hours and its sale curtailed. Moreover, Lady Gaga started a court case because the product's name was too similar to her own.[226]

Before that, a New York art gallery offered visitors cheese made from the breast milk of three women. The Lady Cheese Shop was a four-day art installation by Miriam Simun, meant to raise ethical questions about modern biotechnologies. She hoped that her cheese would make people think twice about the various ways in which the human body has been used as a factory in which blood, hair, sperm, eggs and organs are produced to be harvested by others.[227]

Such questions are no less relevant when talking about other animals – which brings us back to the *mammalia* that Linnaeus (1707–1778) classified the human species as being part of. Of course, it takes the mammal with the biggest brain to come up with the idea of letting adults suck on female breasts for payment.

Like mushrooms in autumn, websites about breasts appear out of nowhere. They teach women sex tricks or give well-meaning advice. They tell less-endowed women to eat lots of fruit: strawberries, pomegranates and bananas are all supposed to contain booby benefits. Breasts themselves are depicted as fruits, from peaches and apples to watermelons. In the creation stories of Judaism, Christianity and Islam, the forbidden fruit with which Eve seduced Adam has always been linked to her seductive breasts. A sixteenth-century Bible illustration depicts Eve offering Adam the apple with her right hand and a breast with her left.

---

226 Cultural Encyclopedia of the Breast pp. 65–66.
227 'Breast Milk Cheese Available At The Lady Cheese Shop' By Joanna Zelman, *Huffington Post*, 24 May 2011.

Eve Seduces Adam by Bernard Salomon, 1561. Museum of Printing and Graphic
Communication, Lyon.

Associating breasts with puddings or cakes is no less popular. In
the French film *La Grande Bouffe* (1973), actor Philippe Noiret
plays the role of a magistrate dying in the arms of a voluptuous
actress while eating a breast-shaped pudding. In contemporary
Japan, the breast is touted as a delicious dessert: two pale mound-
shaped puddings at chest height of a young girl on the package
attract attention; they are packed separately in hard plastic, each
with a pink dot in the middle. Above left is the message: 'Eat
lovingly' and on the right, a warning: 'The cup is fragile, so be
careful.'[228]

---

228 Weird Asia News, 'Japanese Breast Pudding', 12 July 2006. This source has since been
     removed but was originally accessed here: https://weirdasianews.com/2006/12/07/
     japanese-breast-pudding-yummy/.

Japanese supermarket breast-shaped dessert, 2017.

Surf the websites of cosmetic surgeons and positive comments fly in from all sides: 'I LOVE LOVE LOVE my new natural-looking breasts … Go for it!'[229] The English poet Frieda Hughes breaks the vicious circle with a poem about the perfect silicone breasts, the possessor of which does not have to utter a word, because everyone instantly understands their wordless language. Until, in the last stanza of the poem, she takes decisive action:

When at last she made the photo shoot,
She gently placed her breasts
Of shiny plastic flesh
Upon the table for
The cameraman,
And left.[230]

229 This source has since been removed but was originally accessed here: https://www.realself.com/review/miami-fl-breast-augmentation-boob-deprived

230 Frieda Hughes, 'Breasts', from *Out of the Ashes* (Bloodaxe Books, 2018).

Bare breasts in a globalised world

From an international conference on the consequences of globalisation in 2000 in Dar es Salaam, two striking statements by Africans have stayed with me. One was: 'Globalisation is like a medicine: taking too much, you get sick; take too little, you'll die.' The other portrayed the immense power of advertising in a grim simile: 'Globalisation is like rape – you can do nothing about it, so it's best to lean back and enjoy.'

Since the twentieth century, information, products and images have been moving around the world at lightning speed. Western commercial messages have an impact worldwide and the same applies to images of breasts. Less than a century ago, men and women in tropical areas usually walked around naked. Bare breasts were for nursing babies, and that is what the women did without embarrassing anyone – in the market, while working the land or anywhere on the road. Even in regions where breasts were mostly covered because of the cold, children were raised for centuries with the image of mothers with babies on the breast.

Today, ever more working women switch to bottle-feeding when their maternity leave expires, while women breastfeeding their babies in public spaces experience disapproving glances or are made to feel embarrassed in societies where breastfeeding used to be perfectly normal. Erotic advertising images have affected the naturalness of the nourishing breast, not only in the Western world. They spread confusion and reinforce the one-sided way in which men now look at women and women at themselves.

In 2014, Louise Burns discreetly fed her twelve-week-old baby in the dining room of five-star London hotel Claridge's. The floor manager immediately asked her to cover her bosom with a napkin. When Louise posted equally modest before-and-after pictures on Facebook, activist mothers descended on the hotel to stage a public breastfeed protest next to the entrance.[231]

Until recently, breastfeeding was an everyday phenomenon in China. An American researcher wrote in 2000:

> From my research in China, it's very clear that the breast is much less sexualised there than it is in American culture [...]. It's neither hidden nor revealed in any particular way in women's dress or undergarments. In many villages, women sit in the sun with their breasts exposed, and older women will be out washing clothes with their breasts exposed, and it's all completely irrelevant to erotic arousal.[232]

This sounds idyllic, but in contemporary Asia, times are undeniably changing. A Chinese woman who was recently feeding her baby on a crowded train was photographed by a fellow passenger and scandalised on Weibo, the Chinese version of X (formerly Twitter), with the text: 'Let me remind you that this is the Beijing metro and not the bus that runs through your village.' The photo went viral and sparked a furious debate about breastfeeding. Many rejected the mother's behaviour, because she had openly shown her 'sexual organs'. Others defended her and considered it a shame that this intimate photo had been shared on the internet without her permission, among them a doctor who was also a mother: 'Breasts are not sexual organs and babies need to be fed when they are hungry. She is a great mother.' Apparently Chinese citizens find the sight of a baby on the mother's breast in public just as embarrassing as many contemporary Westerners.

---

231   'Claridge's breastfeeding row: Protest by mothers', BBC News, 6 December 2014.
232   Emily Martin, in Angier p. 139.

Africa is changing as rapidly as China. In Nigeria, a young mother, afraid of breastfeeding her baby while using public transport, ended up in an embarrassing situation when she kept pretending nothing was the matter, however much her baby cried. 'Put the baby on the breast or the breast on the baby' – meaning you can solve a problem in more than one way – is a popular Yoruba proverb. Male passengers loudly addressed the young woman, accusing her of being cruel and insensitive. One of them scornfully yelled: 'Why are you trying to deny this child what is naturally his?' And an old man openly wondered: 'What is in your breast that no eyes have seen? I beg you, breastfeed that child!' Only after much pressure did the woman reluctantly give in.[233] Why was she so unwilling to suckle her baby in public? According to the article in the *Vanguard*, this new development is due to advertisers of imported baby milk and the spreading of erotic breast images making educated women refuse their babies their 'natural right'. In all human memory breastfeeding was nothing to be embarrassed about. But the nourishing and seductive functions of breasts have got in each other's way to the point where it's unclear whether one is acceptable in public, or neither.

India is a huge country, and many Indian mothers confirm that breastfeeding is prevalent and not an issue for discussion. Others complain about lurking men who make breastfeeding women feel embarrassed. Here, as in China, there is a great difference between modern city women and village women who routinely take out a breast to feed a child wherever, as soon as it cries. In urbanised areas, upper-class mothers and women with higher education no longer breastfeed in public.[234]

---

233   'Exclusive breast feeding: Whither Nigeria in the campaign?' by Sola Ogundipe & Chioma Obinna, *Vanguard*, 7 August 2011.

234   With the exceptions of the observations in Nigeria and Iran, the citations and commentaries in this paragraph on breastfeeding come from https://www.007b.

An Afghan doctor writes that, in his country, breastfeeding is difficult because Islam demands that women completely cover their bodies, even though in Islamic countries discreet public breastfeeding is permitted. In Iran, headscarves are required, but mothers, with part of the *chador* over their torso and baby, do breastfeed in the streets and on public transport: 'Over here it is not considered a sexual act,' I was told in Tehran, 'but in public, young women are doing it less and less.'

In countries where breastfeeding in public is prohibited, such as Saudi Arabia and the Gulf States, male control over their own desires is challenged. An Indian man shares his experience in the region:

> I was travelling to Dubai on a flight. My baby was being breastfed at the time. My wife was hesitant, but upon seeing the baby crying she started breastfeeding. I covered her and the baby with a newspaper. The guy in the other row was staring like an animal. I wondered how this person could stare so recklessly at a woman who is feeding a baby. I was very angry and at the peak of losing control, I wanted to punch him. But keeping control of myself, I just wondered if someone stared at his own wife's breasts when feeding their baby, what would be his reaction? These guys have to grow up![235]

By contrast, a Saudi from Jeddah is full of empathy for the staring man:

---

com/public-breastfeeding-world.php. This rich and comforting website shows breasts of every kind to make clear that breasts are completely normal body parts and meant to feed babies.

235 'Breastfeeding in public around the world' via 007b, see 'Asia'; 'Breastfeeding Muslim Mothers Support Group, Facebook.

If a woman feeds her baby and the people are seeing
her, of course they like to see her breast more and more
and maybe they become hot and like to do sex with that
lady who is feeding. And I think it is not good that any
lady feed her babies in public places. If she wants, yes,
she can move to the place where no one can see her.[236]

What would this man make of the Icelandic member of parliament
breastfeeding her six-week-old daughter in parliament, when
she was unexpectedly called forward to elaborate on a proposal
she had submitted earlier? The child kept on drinking while the
mother gave the requested explanation. Nobody blinked. In Brazil,
minister Manuela d'Ávila breastfed her baby in the National
Assembly, and in Australia, the House of Representatives recently
changed the house rules so that breastfeeding and bottle-feeding,
previously not permitted, are now allowed.

Activists continue to claim the right to breastfeed in public.
In Hong Kong, a hundred young mothers protested against
the increasing intolerance by feeding their babies in public in a
flash mob. That same weekend in the United States, a group of
female soldiers gathered in front of the Jefferson Monument in
Washington, D.C. dressed in army uniform, breastfeeding their
babies to call attention to the position of young mothers in the
army. Gradually, lactation rooms are being provided, but not
without protests against reluctant superiors. The Facebook page
'Breast-feeding in Combat Boots,' reflects that the majority of
young mothers in the army run into structural barriers. [237]

Are women more respected in societies where the breast is
seen as a powerful symbol of nurturing and loving care than in

---

236   *Ibid.*
237   Breastfeeding   in   Combat   Boots   website,   available   here: https://
      breastfeedingincombatboots.com/.

societies where the breast is only seen as an erotic object? Asks Margaret Miles, author of *A Complex Delight*.[238] A relevant question in an age where breasts in advertising automatically land in the brain folder of eroticism and sex. No one thinks of a nurturing mother when a woman pops a breast out of her elegant dress in an advert or a tabloid snap. However, going back in time, one does find early examples of that same seduction device. For example, in the Church of the Holy Sepulchre of Barletta in southern Italy, where an early medieval mural shows three beautiful women doing their utmost to seduce Saint Anthony by each offering him an attractive right breast. Having courageously resisted temptation, he was rewarded with sanctification. Back then Satan exploited the female appearance with all his might to seduce believers, and nowadays it's the media. Nothing new, except for the global scale.

The Temptation of Saint Anthony. Mural, Barletta Basilica Santo Sepulchro, Italy. 1200 – 1300 CE.

---

238   Miles: Afterword.

PART III

POWER AND POWERLESSNESS

Saint Agatha of Sicily being tortured. Royal Library, The Hague. Medieval manuscript, c. 1390-400.

CHAPTER NINE

BEAT YOUR WIFE, SHE WILL KNOW WHY

Oh, Saint Agatha, who withstood the unwelcome
advances from unwanted suitors,
and suffered pain and torture
for your devotion to Our Lord,
we celebrate your faith, dignity and martyrdom.
Protect us against rape and other violations,
guard us against breast cancer
and other afflictions of women,
and inspire us to overcome adversity.
(Prayer to Saint Agatha)

If the male organ rises up, it is an overwhelming
catastrophe, for once provoked it cannot be resisted
by either reason or religion. For this organ is more
powerful than all the instruments used by Satan
against man.
(Ibn Abbas)

THE HUMAN WEAKNESS of violence against women stems from the fact that men were usually physically stronger and developed more muscle strength through hunting, while women, pregnant or surrounded by children, depended on a 'protector'.

'Beat your wife regularly, if you don't know why, she will know why' is still a popular proverb in West Africa. I heard it for the first time jokingly quoted in Dakar where my Wolof translator assured me it was of Arab origin. A similar European example is the Iberian message: 'To keep your wife on the rails, hit her, and if she derails, hit her.' Introduced to America long ago by Spanish settlers, it smoothly transitioned into Puerto Rico's oral tradition. Violence against women has been unabashedly promoted in proverbs from almost everywhere:

> For whom beats up his wife, God improves the food. (Russian)

> Women and cutlets, the more you beat them, the more succulent they become. (German)

> A woman, a dog and a walnut tree, the more you beat them, the better they be. (Western Europe and United States)

> Clubbing produces virtuous wives. (Chinese)

> The nails of a cart and the head of a woman only work when they are hit hard. (Rajasthani, India)[239]

> A beaten woman is going to be a better wife. (Korean)

---

239 For proverbial violence, see Chapter 4 in *Never Marry a Woman with Big Feet*. For worldwide proverbs about violence, see www.womeninproverbsworldwide.com.

Male violence against women appears to exist everywhere around the world. We have also seen how fear of women's uncontrollable sexuality and birth-giving capacity gives rise to the male urge to have control over the womb – because it is presumed that, without male intervention, the world would be in chaos.

From a phallic perspective

As long as the fertile earth was represented by female gods or autonomously creating goddesses, vulvas were honoured not only for their life-creating powers, but also for their magical protective effect in times of calamity. For a better understanding of historical developments, some attention to the phallus must be paid here.

It is estimated that the worship of the erect penis began in the prehistoric New Stone Age (around 11,000 BCE). In cultures where tributes to the penis prevailed, not only did stories circulate about penis gods, but penis images were erected – at home, in the courtyard, in temples and on the street. In myths, the phallus often took on the size of an elephant's trunk, as with the Aboriginal Djanggawul. Nor was the Egyptian God Atum poorly endowed. A bas-relief on an excavated temple wall depicts him in the acrobatic act of autofellatio, lying on his back with his feet above his head, about to take his extremely long phallus in his mouth. The Chinese emperor Zhou Xin (1105–1046 BCE) had such a potent penis that he could allegedly walk around a room with a naked woman perched on his erection.[240]

There is no shortage of such stories, nor images. Hindus worship phallus-shaped stones, columns or pillars representing the creative power of the god Shiva; and in Dorset, England, the Cerne Abbas

---

240   Maggie Paley, *The Book of the Penis*, 1999 pp. 41–44.

Giant is a sight to behold: a 180-foot-tall limestone outline of a giant wielding a bludgeon in his right hand and an erection up to his ribs. He is so impressive that many people climb up the hill specifically to have sex on top of the phallus. Widely believed to date to prehistoric or Roman times, after extensive research in May 2021, the National Trust concluded that creation of the Cerne Abbas Giant actually dates from the late Saxon period (700–1100 CE).[241]

Penis festivals are still celebrated in various countries. For example, a giant phallus is carried on participants' shoulders in a predominantly male parade during the annual Festival of the Steel Phallus in Japan. At the Holi Festival in Rajasthan, India, a giant phallus is carried around in honour of the local god Eloji. The crowd attending the festival mainly consists of men singing songs in praise of Eloji to stimulate their own virility, but women who want to become pregnant with a male child also venerate Eloji. This god dedicated to sex is depicted as a man with an extravagant moustache and an unnaturally long penis.[242]

Ancient Greek stories and images confirm the public attention the penis enjoyed. In everyday life the phallus was well represented in the streets of Athens thanks to the *herms*, named after the god Hermes: a stone base with a sculpted head, two testicles and an erect penis. They were found in front of private houses and marked the boundaries of public and private areas.[243] Here, too, men carried a giant phallus in procession, as can be seen on painted vases.

241 'Cerne Giant' via National Trust website.
242 Further festival examples were available on https://www.scoopwhoop.com/ Places-Where- Penis-Is-Worshipped/#.5anbkposd; https://www.newsflare.com/ video/189888/ but unfortunately these sites have since been removed.
243 Eva C. Keuls, *The Reign of the Phallus*, 1985:385ff.

Left: Cerne Abbas Giant, Dorset, England, *c.* 700–1100 CE.

Right: Archaic herm with exceptionally intact phallus, Siphnos, Greece, *c.* 520 BCE.

Eva Keuls defines phallocracy as a prevailing principle in which 'the human race is essentially male, the female being a mere adjunct, unfortunately required for the purpose of reproduction. The natural consequence of this notion is the elimination of the female from all social processes.'[244] She describes the power of the phallus among the ancient Greeks as a cultural system in which the penis is not represented as an organ of unification or a means of mutual pleasure, but as a weapon:

> [...] a spear or war club, and a scepter of sovereignty. In sexual terms, phallocracy takes such forms as rape, disregard of the sexual satisfaction of women, and access

244   *Ibid.* pp. 86–87.

to the bodies of prostitutes who are literally enslaved or allowed no other means of support. In the political sphere, it spells imperialism and patriarchal behaviour in civic affairs.[245]

Greek tradition has stories about the struggle of Greek heroes against the Amazons. These warrior women – according to some their society consisted exclusively of women – were independent and bellicose. Classical images depict Greek heroes slashing and clubbing Amazons to death or chasing them away.

Occasionally, an Amazon threateningly aims her lance at the genitals of a naked Greek man such as Theseus, Athens' hero, but that is quite exceptional. Yet such scenes suggest the threat of a possible defeat, says Keuls, and unmistakably reflect male fear of female rebellion, as well as the possibility of a weakening of power. Even though the phallus held sway, obsessive fear of women always persisted, and men never sat easily on the throne.[246] Is this not the thief's fear that someone will one day ransack his own house?

Political, cultural and religious traditions are still tormented by this tension between power and fear. Thousands of proverbs have been thought up to allay male fear with stereotypical perceptions of the perfect wife: smaller and younger than him, less talented and less educated.[247] The fear of insecure men easily turns into anger, often escalating into verbal or physical violence. Many men have internalised belittling messages about women all their lives, swallowing the warning that these unreliable creatures must be strictly controlled to prevent chaos.

---

245   *Ibid.* 2.
246   *Ibid.* 3ff. In her research she compared more than eight hundred images of Amazons in Greek antiquity, especially in Athens. Amazon stories belong to the large category of myths in which a country or the entire world was populated by women only.
247   Cf. *Never Marry a Woman with Big Feet*, Chapter 4.

Greek warrior in battle with an Amazon queen, painted on an amphora, Walters Art Museum, Baltimore, *c.* 500–490 BCE.

This makes it difficult to approach someone of the other sex without prejudice. For centuries, the dominant narrative was that a ready-made person existed within male sperm, and the man's role was to introduce it into a womb. It is in this context that many men believed – and continue to believe – that women contribute little or nothing to society, or even to their own pregnancy.

The second quote opening this chapter, provided by a respected companion of the Prophet Muhammad, has often been quoted approvingly. Ibn Abbas reveals a formidable fear of the unpredictable behaviour of the most sensitive male body part, while the continuation of his statement, in which he directly addresses women, is no less revealing: 'That is why the Prophet, Allah's peace be upon him, said, "I have not seen creatures lacking in reason and religious commitment more able of overcoming men of reason and wisdom than you."' His line of reasoning is much older than Islam, and is still eagerly practised in all contexts where marginalising women remains the order of things.

Myths, religion and popular culture influence the way in which we look at ourselves and at the other sex. The fact that a man is not responsible for controlling his own drives is a perverse misunderstanding that enjoys unprecedented authority.

This rather grievous misconception about the male sex has become so ingrained that lack of self-control is confused with 'masculinity'. A man's best remedy for arousal by a female stranger was to rush home and 'discharge the material of that excitement where it rightfully belongs, so that Satan [...] does not entangle him in sin' – advice originating from the writings of Imam Muslim (Muslim Ibn al-Hajjaj, 821–875). Over the centuries this misconception has grown rather than shrunk. Whereas in the past this message was widely transmitted in oral traditions and written texts, today on YouTube, ultra-orthodox preachers repeat the warning to women that their prayers will not be answered if they do not immediately oblige their husbands when they come home agitated and in need of their wives.[248] A professor specialising in the philosophy of law was also inclined to sympathise with the ideas of Ibn Abbas in a column about the Harvey Weinstein affair, even though he himself is a dogmatic atheist:

> Such a situation – alone with a woman in a room – remains a temptation for many men. Their hormones may strike up, so that their will follows their desire instead of their reason. Irrevocably this will lead to unsavory things. That is why it is better to prevent something like this from happening. Hence, women were supposed to keep their distance from foreign

---

248   Hoqoq az-zawdj deel 2 (rechten van de man) - aboe Chayma amazigh dutch nl' via YouTube, 2011 (in Arabic and Dutch); popular preachers such as Al-Qaradawi spread the same message.

men – that is, any man who is not a husband or brother – and if a tête-à-tête was unavoidable, to take along a trustworthy male. It seems to me that this line of thought was certainly not entirely wrong.[249]

In this way he automatically puts the solution back on to the woman's plate. Just like in the time of Ibn Abbas, it is better for women to be guided. Wouldn't it by now be more reasonable for an adult man who is afraid his hormones might play up – for example, during a thesis meeting with an attractive student – to get himself a testosterone supervisor?

The 'effects' of testosterone continue to be based more on popular opinion than on scientific evidence. In Cordelia Fine's *Testosterone Rex* (2017) she argues that the whole testosterone fable was invalidated a long time ago. Or, in the words of University of Amsterdam professor of sexology Ellen Laan: 'There is not one piece of evidence proving that men who conduct nonconsensual sexual behaviour have more testosterone than those who do not.'[250]

The devouring mother

Different origin myths have the first ancestors breaking out from a vessel, gourd, bottle, pot or egg. In each version, the womb metaphor refers to both fertile fullness and greedy threat. In her book *La mère dévorante*, Denise Paulme analyses African story variants on the topic of an uncontrollable gourd, which swallows everything and everyone until a ram succeeds in cleaving the

---

249 Andreas Kinneging about Weinstein and the well-considered will, in *Novum*, April 2018.
250 Interview in *NRC-Handelsblad*, 17 November 2017. See also: Van Lunsen and Laan, *Seks! Een leven lang leren* (*Sex! A Lifelong Education*), 2017.

gluttonous monster with a powerful headbutt and frees all the living beings locked up inside.

In a positive sense, the gourd symbolises the ideal mother, but the female pregnancy experience also gives rise to male need for compensation. The alarming gluttony of the gourd can only be annihilated by a redeeming 'outside' male element – a virile ram or muscular lumberjack,[251] echoing how male superiority is mainly displayed outside the home 'in the domain of public life from which women are preferably excluded.' Such stories are full of incidents or dramas in which male order overcomes chaos, which is attributed to women.[252]

Despite different cultural and religious backgrounds, quite similar restrictions have been imposed on the physical presence and appearance of women throughout history.[253] There has been a spectacular increase in the covering of the female body between 1500 and 1900, especially in areas where people do not need any body covering to protect themselves against the cold. That increase is mainly due to influences from outside: Islamic conquests or Christian missionary zeal, and colonial occupation combined with a compulsory drive for 'civilisation'. Globalisation makes visible the extent to which societies are open to change or rather cherish local traditions. It is evident that political, religious and commercial authorities make use of dress to confirm, debate or overturn existing power relations in favour of their own impact. Wherever sex differences are emphasised, fear of equality is lurking around the corner.

---

251   Denise Paulme, *La mère dévorante*, (*Journal des Africanistes*: 1975).

252   Paulme: 282; Héritier II pp. 131–132.

253   For limitations in freedom to move or being harassed in the public space: see the Womanstats overview about women's mobility, and the many religious and/or commercial rules for women's more or less obligatory covering or uncovering the body, as explained in my earlier book Naked or Covered, A History of Dressing and Undressing Around the World (2017).

Traditionally, fertile women have been restricted in multiple ways, whereas post menopause, women had more freedom and were sometimes even allowed to 'drink beer like a man', as a Ganda proverb used to define the difference.

Breast rippers and other instruments of torture

Male aggression is often directed at parts of the body that men themselves don't possess, as can be concluded from a rather sad litany of information about mutilation and rape. In *De Vrouw in Natuuren Volkenkunde* (*The Woman in Physics and Ethnology*, published at the beginning of the twentieth century), the authors depict gruesome traditions of breast mutilation – unfortunately without explaining the underlying motives:

> In Australia, the nipples of young girls are pulled out to make suckling impossible. Even in the last century there was a horrific mutilation in the Christian sect of the Copts in Russia [in which] the nipples of ten-, nine- and even seven-year-old girls were cut off; and when the case came to court, these children obstinately persisted that they had inflicted this mutilation on themselves [...]. Apparently, the sacrament played a major role in their religion. Instead of the host, they were given a small piece of bleeding girl's breast.

This may look unbelievable, but the book includes illustrations.

Coptic girl, about twenty years old,
with mutilated breasts. Engraving, late
nineteenth century.[254]

In Christian legends about saints, 'pagan' rulers assault beautiful
and pious girls who end up as devout martyrs. An early example
is provided in multiple stories about Saint Agatha (*c.* 231–251),
whose martyrdom was popularised by Saint Jerome and others
in the sixth century. Agatha was born in Catania or Palermo in
Sicily and became one of the first canonised Christians. After
this exemplary virgin of noble descent rejected the advances of
the Roman governor and refused to marry him, he tortured her
to death:

> During these tortures she prayed: 'For love of chastity
> I am made to hang from a rack. Help me, O Lord my
> God, as they knife my breasts.' Agatha rebuked the
> governor for his barbarity: 'Godless, cruel, infamous
> tyrant, are you not ashamed to despoil a woman of that
> by which your own mother nursed you?'[255]

---

254   In Ploss and Bartels, 1912.
255   See 'Memorial of St. Agatha, virgin and martyr' via Catholic Culture online.

Agatha died from the consequences of her torments. The patron saint of breast cancer patients, rape victims and wet-nurses, women in desperate situations still call on her in prayer. The main symbols of Saint Agatha are breasts on a dish – drawings and paintings depict her bearing her own severed breasts on a silver platter or holding in one hand the pincers gripping one of her breasts. An illustration in a medieval manuscript shows two men each ripping off a breast from her frail body.

On 5 February, Saint Agatha's feast day, a procession carries her life-size statue, ornamented with a wealth of jewellery, through the streets of Catania, surrounded by thousands of people crying, moaning and invoking her. Sicilians indulge in a traditional sweet spongy pastry in the shape of a virginal breast covered with a crunchy icing and topped with a candied red cherry to keep the memory of Saint Agatha's cruel fate fresh in the mind. Originally made by nuns, these *minni di virgini* are readily available today throughout Sicily at numerous delicatessens.

Cassatella di sant'Agata or *minni di virgini*, Cantania, Sicily (Stefano Mortello).

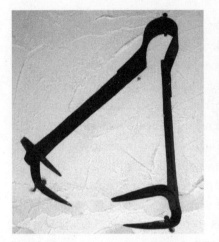 

Medieval instruments to torture women. Left: Breast Ripper. Foltermuseum, Freiburg;
right: Pear of Anguish. Fortress Museum, Salzburg.

It is apparent from the iron instruments of torture displayed in
museums that torture by the rack did happen, and is not only the
imagery of stories. In Europe, during the Middle Ages, torture
instruments were especially invented for breasts or wombs. The
breast ripper, which consisted of iron pincers with claws, was
either used cold or red-hot to brand the exposed breasts of an
unmarried mother or to put pressure on a female suspect accused
of blasphemy, heresy, adultery or abortion:

> Used as a way to punish women, the breast ripper was
> a painful and cruel way to mutilate a woman's breasts.
> [...] A common variant of the breast ripper is often
> referred to as 'The Spider', which is a similar instrument
> attached to a wall. The victim's breasts were fixed to the
> claws and the woman was pulled by the torturer away
> from the wall; successfully removing them.[256]

---

256   See 'breast ripper' via Medieval Reality website.

A woman forced to undergo this torture was horribly disfigured for the rest of her life, if she survived.

Another torture instrument especially designed for use on women's bodies was the 'pear of anguish'. A small version was applied to the mouth or anus of men; a larger model was pushed through a woman's vagina into her womb. From the outside, a screw was tightened further and further, as a result of which the sharp blades of this pear-shaped instrument swung open internally. Torture with the pear irremediably maimed the affected cavity, almost always with a fatal outcome.

Aggression against breasts, wombs and genitals still occurs – and not only in porn fantasies. In areas of Syria and Iraq where IS prevailed, Christian and Yezidi girls were raped and tortured by their so-called owners, who treated them as sex slaves. According to ISIS fighters' interpretation of the Quran, raping a slave was not a sin. They even did their prayers before starting.[257]

An extreme seventeenth-century example of sexual violence as a weapon of war against women was recorded by the Dutch traveller Jan Janszoon Struys. Struys was working on building the Russian tsar's fleet in Astrakhan. One day, the city was besieged by Cossacks. A Muslim Khan, who was a vassal of the Shah of Persia, prevailed and Struys was captured in Dagestan and became a slave. In his book *Drie Aanmerkelijke en seer Rampspoedige Reysen* (*Three Considerable and Very Disastrous Travels*, Amsterdam, 1676), Struys reported a shocking incident that took place during this time. A Polish concubine of a Persian trader managed to escape to the Polish consulate. The Khan gave the trader permission to get the girl back and 'do with her whatever he wanted.' He chose to skin her alive and drape her

---

257 Callimachi, Rukmini, 'ISIS Enshrines a Theology of rape,' *New York Times*, 13 August 2015.

stripped skin on the wall of a room as a warning to all his other concubines.

In 1673, Struys returned to the Netherlands as a free man and commented on this tragic event in his travel story: 'Even though they are the dirtiest, most horny and unfaithful men, they still want their wives to be honest, chaste and faithful.' A lifelike engraving of the woman's horrific torture was included in his book. On the right of the image, the woman is tied down in preparation for the skinning; being stripped off, her clothes and slippers strewn on the floor. In the room next door, the Persian trader explains to his assembled concubines that a similar fate awaits them, should they ever attempt to escape.[258]

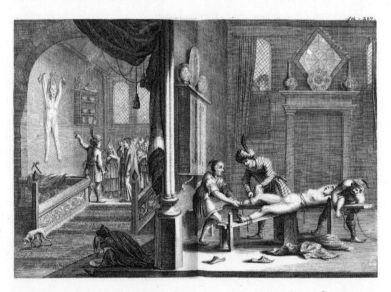

From Jan Janszoon Struys' *Drie Aanmerkelijke en seer Rampspoedige Reysen*. Copper engraving, 1676. Leiden University Libraries.

---

258   Jan Janszoon Struys, *Drie Aanmerkelijke en seer Rampspoedige Reysen*. Amsterdam: 1676; re-issue: 2014. With thanks to Arnoud Vrolijk, curator Eastern Manuscripts, Leiden University Libraries.

In the same period, no less gruesome tortures were occurring across Europe. Women accused of witchcraft frequently had their breasts cut off before they were burned at the stake. An ill-famed case is the history of the Bavarian Pappenheimer family, itinerant latrine cleaners. Before mother Anna was burned as a witch, executioners cut off her breasts and stuffed them first in her own mouth and then in those of her two sons to ridicule her role as mother.

Everywhere in the world mothers of adolescent girls worry about men who cannot be trusted to keep their hands off their children. Concerned about the wellbeing of their daughters, mothers sometimes carry out disastrous acts of torture themselves to prevent worse scenarios. One of those security measures is the tradition of 'breast ironing', which occurs in rural areas of Cameroon and some other African countries:

> Breast ironing is a breast-flattening practice performed on adolescent girls by applying a firm pressure massage with hot objects, such as stones, coconut shells, pestles, spoons and even hammers. Application of hot fruit peels and tight chest binding to make the girl's chest look flat usually follow the massage.[259]

As with infibulation and clitoridectomy, mothers, aunts or grandmothers take control over the bodies of the girls in their families in matters of breast ironing. The intentions are good: by means of breast mutilation the mothers try to make their daughters less sexually attractive to protect them against assault and rape, HIV infection and unwanted pregnancy, in the hope that they will stay longer in school and be able to take care of

---

259 *Cultural Encyclopedia of the Breast*: 68ff.

themselves and their children in future life. Nevertheless, this practice produces mainly negative effects, including painful blisters, infections, abscesses, damage to the mammary glands, unsightly scars and post-traumatic stress.[260] In some areas, more than half the girls undergo this dangerous treatment. Campaigns for abolition are carried out intermittently, but there is still no law prohibiting this harmful tradition.

Countries where the practice is believed to occur include Benin, Burkina Faso, Cameroon, the Central African Republic, Chad, Côte d'Ivoire, Guinea-Bissau, Guinea-Conakry, Kenya, Nigeria, South Africa, Togo and Zimbabwe. In recent years there have been a number of news reports of the practice occurring within immigrant communities in the United Kingdom. [...] Due to migration, it is quite likely that breast ironing is being practised among African diaspora populations in the West (e.g, North America and Western Europe).[261]

Rape is a constant throughout history. All the previously outlined examples of aggression against girls and women took place in situations outside of armed conflicts but during wartime, insecurity is dramatically magnified, and rape is turned into a weapon. Women and children have always been easy prey for objectionable sexual behaviour in military conflicts. In the former Roman settlement of Cornelia on the Neckar in present-day Germany, the Huns under the command of Attila (406–453) killed all the men, then raped the women before cutting off their breasts. The town later became known as Wimpfen, a

---

260 'Cameroon's Women Call Time On Breast Ironing' by Amy Hall, *New Internationalist*, 1 May 2013.

261 Unfortunately, this article has subsequently been removed but was originally available at https://newint.org/features/2013/05/01/tales-of-taboo/;.https://www.ncbi.nlm.nih.gov/pmc/articles/PMC8005301/. In recent years a number of news reports refer to this practice occurring within immigrant communities in the United Kingdom.

corruption of the German word *Weiberpein*, meaning 'women's pain'.

Such offences also occurred in recent history. Towards the end of World War II, soldiers of the Red Army raped one hundred thousand women en route to Berlin. Serial rape is a disastrous weapon that deeply humiliates not only the victims but also their families, as a raped woman was seen as a tarnished woman.[262] Convinced that they had lost their honour, the girls were encouraged (often by their own fathers) to commit suicide; hundreds did. Men whose wives were victims sometimes killed their entire family and then themselves.

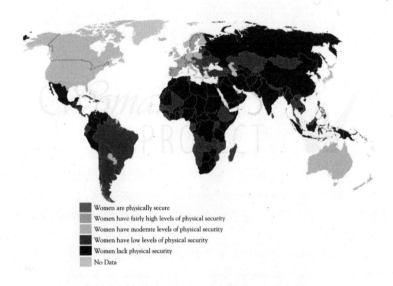

Women are physically secure
Women have fairly high levels of physical security
Women have moderate levels of physical security
Women have low levels of physical security
Women lack physical security
No Data

Map showing the physical security of women, globally, 2014.

---

262   Jolande Withuis in *Trouw*, 25 November 2017.

Detesting one's own body

The perception that their body does not meet the 'ideal' form and norm makes women work harder on their appearance than men. How 'natural' female appearance looks in Western societies depends on the context and situation:

> ['Natural' features] are best tolerated in periods when the distribution of gender roles is most self-evident: the women at home, the men outside. The very conservative [European] 1950s still loved plump creatures. Conversely, when women venture into traditionally masculine territories and occupy a larger place in social life, it seems as if they have to make up for the resulting imbalance by reducing the place that their bodies occupy in that very space.[263]

Since the motherly, nourishing female body has historically been associated with or imprisoned in the domestic environment, it looks as if women needed a different type of body to escape from the bonds of history. This adjusted into a body that could not be associated with women's envy-evoking ability to reproduce. The maternal plump body was revoked in favour of looking 'like a boy with small breasts,' in the words of a psychiatrist specialising in eating disorders.

Contemporary stories about bone-thin girls show a new variant of unconditional female submission to a condition of being looked at and acted upon instead of looking and acting in the world by themselves.[264] Some agencies warn young models

---

263   *Ibid.* p. 148, referring to Susan Bordo's *Unbearable Weight*.
264   *Ibid.* p. 149.

starting to develop hips and breasts to beware: 'you are becoming a woman'.

The ideal contours of contemporary female models, stimulating anorexia, are reminiscent of the ascetic practices to which exemplary girls and women in the first centuries of Christianity surrendered to gain respect. At the time, fasting was highly recommended to promote chastity, but women took refusing food as a new way to boost their low-value status. Some went so far that their breasts shrivelled and menstruation stopped. By wiping out their feminine forms, they became physically more like men, vainly deluding themselves that they would finally be treated as equals in society, as fourth-century bishop and theologian Basil of Ancyra had promised:

> Although clothed in a female body, they have by means of asceticism beaten off the shape engendered from it for the sake of the soul, and have made themselves appear like men through excellence, just as their souls have been created equal. And just as men, through asceticism, pass from men to the rank of angels, so also these women, through asceticism, pass from women to the same rank as theirs.[265]

However, to prevent misunderstandings, the bishop immediately added that equality in earthly life held only for the soul, but in the afterlife both sexes would become 'equal in all ways'. The desperate perspective of anorexia sufferers reminds us of the impossible efforts of their ascetic predecessors. The message is irrevocable: you may try your best to lose your female shape and appearance and functions out of self-loathing, but you will remain a second-

---

265   Quoted in Theresa Shaw, p. 237.

class citizen as long as you are trapped in a female body. Medieval ascetic women – some have even been sanctified – served as an example to ordinary women who continued to eat and to bleed when they were not pregnant. Just like in contemporary society, the promoted image of extremely thin ascetic girls without female qualities went hand in hand with negative images of women in society.[266]

The brain

Knowledge and learning has always been important. Knowledge is power, knowledge is wealth, knowledge means prestige and privilege, according to worldwide traditional wisdom. Men took that glowing recommendation to heart while withholding this fervently desired knowledge from women, claiming this was to protect their virtue:

> The glory of man is knowledge, the glory of woman is to renounce it. (Portuguese, Brazil)

> Men should set knowledge before virtue, women virtue before knowledge. (German)

> Virtuous is a woman without knowledge. (Chinese, Taiwan)

On the one hand, women's brainpower was denied or scorned:

---

266   *Ibid.* More extensive information about negativity towards women's appearance in the Western tradition in Umberto Eco's *History of Ugliness*, Chapter 4.

A wise woman is twice a fool. (English)

The women's side of the house: the side without knowledge. (Burmese)

On the other hand, society was warned about the inherent dangers of female intelligence. Even in the oldest known sources men are advised that clever and capable women are to be condemned:

A woman's intelligence can cause a catastrophe. (Sanskrit)

A man doesn't want a woman smarter than he is. (English)

A dog is smarter than a woman, it does not bark at its master. (Russian)

To educate a woman is like putting a knife in the hands of a monkey. (Hindi/Portuguese)

A crowing hen and a woman who knows Latin never come to a good end. (German/Spanish)

Women ought to be silent in the presence of men. Showing knowledge as a woman was unusual and inappropriate, and public success was presented as an unwanted feminine feature.

Obstacles against university-educated women remained insurmountably high, and often, they still are. If no restrictive laws existed, male researchers concluded that women were unable to perform intellectually – the fact their skull contained fewer brain cells than a man's made them unsuitable for an academic education. In his book *Sex and Education; or, a Fair Chance for Girls* (1875) Edward H. Clarke argues that 'the brain cannot take more than its share without injury to other organs. It cannot do more than its share without depriving other organs.' Therefore, he claims that while girls can go to school and study as boys do, this will cause them to suffer from 'euralgia, uterine disease, hysteria, and other derangements of the nervous system'. Moreover, he refers to worrisome cases wherein small-breasted, scholarly women had been unable to nurse their own babies and forced to resort to wet-nurses or bottle-feeding.[267]

As more girls went to university, some scholars kept insisting that for women, study was 'unnatural'; it caused sterility and perversity. In the nineteenth century, it was suggested that a woman's ovaries would shrivel up as soon as she received higher education. In the twentieth century, women in Saudi Arabia were told that their ovaries would shrink if they drove a car. The ban on women driving a car was nonetheless lifted in 2018. Of course, girls were – and still are, whether or not jokingly – warned that by studying they would lose their chances of finding a husband, a woman's main objective in life. In short, a learned woman was a lost woman.

Although arguments about the inferior female brain have been outdated for over a century, some ultra-orthodox Muslim clerics cling in vain to the notion that women's bodies prevent wisdom:

> No sensible person can deny the fact that man, due to
> his innate capabilities, is superior to them in so many
> things. The poor woman passes through such periods or

---

267   Edward H. Clarke, *Sex in Education; or, A Fair Chance for Girls*, pp. 7 and 43, https://www.gutenberg.org/cache/epub/18504/pg18504-images.html.

intervals in her life in which she is almost incapable of
doing anything and has to look to others for help and
cooperation. These periods are romances, pregnancy,
bleeding after childbirth and suckling the baby.[268]

Arguments that do their utmost to prove that women are at an
intellectual disadvantage have everything to do with the fear of
losing an established order. To effectively exclude women, the
common message 'keep off, keep off' was directly connected with
the female body, as expressed in the Ethiopian Oromo proverb:
'Breasts that contain milk, do not contain intelligence.'

Ironic, then, that despite all efforts to prevent women from
entering classrooms, so many universities, particularly in Europe,
opt for the image of the nourishing mother as their academic
emblem. In 1088, the year of its foundation, the University of
Bologna was the first to choose *Alma Mater Studiorum* as its
motto. Others followed. At the entrance of the Cuban University
of Havana, the words 'Alma Mater' are chiselled in heavy letters
beneath a colossal black marble statue of a woman with open
arms and impressive breasts. Leiden University's Alma Mater
has a chastely covered and inconspicuous bosom, but *Alma
Mater Cantabrigia*, from 1600, presents a dynamic female figure
with rounded breasts, flowing hair and wide-open arms. In
her left hand she holds a sacred cup and in her right hand the
sun of science spreads its shining light. She effortlessly carries
Cambridge's city walls as a crown on her head.

From those breasts bursting with knowledge, for centuries
only students with no breasts of their own benefited – apart from
a few notorious exceptions. In thirteenth-century Italy, Bettisia
Gozzadini put on men's clothes, attended the University of

---

268   Mufti Zaferruddin Miftahi, *Modesty and Chastity in Islam*, 1993 p. 160.

Bologna and graduated more dazzlingly than all her classmates. Against all prejudices, she proved that a woman could become a lawyer. In 1296 she even taught law at her Alma Mater – but that had to be from behind a curtain, lest her beauty distract the attention of her male students.

Only since the twentieth century have European Alma Maters been widely sharing their knowledge with daughters as well as with sons. Graduates the world over still call their university their Alma Mater and themselves her *alumni*, literally meaning 'sucklings'.

Much has changed for the better, but what about at the top level in science? There are still considerably more male professors than female. In 2013 the American Physical Society published an article about the harrowing discrepancy between the number of male and female Nobel laureates in physics: 196 versus just two. The most famous female laureate is Marie Curie, to whom that honour was awarded together with her husband in 1903 for the discovery and investigation of radioactivity. It wasn't until 1972 that a second female physicist was awarded the Nobel Prize in her field: Maria Goeppert Mayer who, for almost all her active life, remained unpaid for her work.[269]

After the death of her husband, Marie Curie won a second Nobel Prize in 1911 for her research in chemistry. In 1910 she was nominated as a member of the French Academy of Sciences. After a heated debate, her male counter-candidate was elected; the difference was two votes and the vote had to be done over.

---

269 The only Nobel Prize category with fewer women is Economics, with one female winner to date – Elinor Ostrom in 2009: see Wikipedia 'female laureates'. With thanks for this information to Dr Hans Goedbloed, Emeritus Professor of Theoretical Plasma Physics, Utrecht University.

The Academy then voted against the admission of women with an overwhelming majority. Even after Marie Curie's second Nobel Prize, the Academy stayed with their decision. The first woman was not allowed to join this illustrious club until 1979. Meanwhile in the UK, before 1945, the only woman in the Royal Society was a skeleton in the anatomical collection.

Hoped-for male progeny: embryo on an imaginary umbilical cord inside a female body. Etching of a painted and carved door, New Guinea.[270]

---

270   In de Clercq and Schmelz, 1893.

CHAPTER TEN

LESSONS FROM THE PAST

The elder Sister said: 'We have really lost nothing, for we remember it all. Let them have that small part. For aren't we still sacred? […] We still have our wombs, don't we?' And the younger Sister agreed with her.
(Wulamba origin myth)

A whole night of labour and then only a daughter.
(Spanish proverb)

A LACK OF the characteristics of the other sex can be experienced as especially harrowing in societies where one sex is more valued or enjoys more privileges than the other. In their morning prayer, orthodox Jewish men openly express their gratitude: 'Blessed are you, Lord our God, Ruler of the Universe, who has not made me a woman.' A common Kurdish saying observes that 'it is better to be a man for one day than a woman for ten days.' A woman I interviewed from Bhutan agrees: 'Being born a woman means a wasted life', and 'I won't come back female' is an old Ashanti saying in southern Ghana, reflecting women's hopes for a better position in a next life. Most oral traditions reflect a gender hierarchy in which it is self-evident who are to be the speakers and who are the silent ones, the keepers of knowledge and the ignorant, the travellers and those staying at home – as if this were the irreversible natural order of things.

The chaos of life involves ambivalent us–them relationships, in which differences are more often emphasised than similarities – differences in gender, language, culture, colour, class, religion and so on. Even from a young age, girls and boys compare their differences and sometimes envy each other, or wonder why they can't have both a penis and a vagina. Thanks to Freud, penis envy has become a popular concept, but womb envy has also been demonstrated to exist.

Oh no, it's a girl

The image from New Guinea that opens this chapter reflects the widespread traditional view that a baby boy is more welcome than a baby girl, a view probably as old as patriarchy. Some four thousand years ago that view was already popular, as evidenced in auspicious and inauspicious omens preserved in cuneiform script on Mesopotamian clay tablets:

If a man's penis is long and thick, he will have sons.
If a woman's nose is symmetrical, [she will give birth
    to] sons.
If a man has sex with a woman on fallow land, she will

give birth to a daughter; if he sleeps with her in a
field or garden [on cultivated land], then she will
give birth to a son.[271]

A girl, finally, a girl! Cartoon,
origin unknown. Late
twentieth century.

For various reasons, the birth of a son has often been greeted with
considerably more enthusiasm than that of a daughter. Preference
for children of a specific gender is not only related to the structure
of society and traditional access to sources of income, but also to
obstinate ideas (whether religiously inspired or not) putting men
'naturally' on a higher plane than women. In the Western world,
there has been a tendency to think that the birth of girls was
due to a lack of virility – thanks in part to the lasting influence
of reliable old sexist Aristotle. In his famous work on animals,
written between 347 and 322 BCE, the philosopher provided
the world with powerful statements about the huge differences
between men and women:

For females are weaker and colder in nature [than
males], and we must look upon the female character as

271   With thanks for personal information to Assyriologist Marten Stol.

being a sort of natural deficiency. Accordingly, while it is within the mother it develops slowly because of its coldness (for development is concoction, and it is heat that concocts, and what is hotter is easily concocted); but after birth it quickly arrives at maturity and old age on account of its weakness, for all inferior things come sooner to their perfection or end, and as this is true of works of art so it is of what is formed by Nature.[272]

Whether or not inspired by this or the work of other Greek philosophers, Western physicians and scholars continued to conduct empirical research, with perspectives often demonstrably clouded by their own bias. Thanks to traditionally cherished ideas, the female body was portrayed as a deviation from the 'norm', or as a less perfect or inferior variant of the male.

Left: *Alma Mater, Havana* by Mario Karbel, 1919.
Right: *Alma Mater Cantabrigia* by John Legate, 1600.

272 Aristotle, *On the Generation of Animals*, Book Four, 6. Translation from the Greek: eBooks University of Adelaide, Australia.

In many cultures, a preference for sons is passed down through the generations and centuries, so that globally, many mothers today still derive their highest achievable social prestige from giving birth to boys. European women themselves are also brainwashed by that wish-for-a-son mentality, as expressed in proverbs, for example:

> He who leaves a boy behind is not really dead. (Danish)

> Many sons, many blessings of God; many daughters, many calamities. (German)

> When a girl is born, even the roofs cry. (Bulgarian)

> When a wife gives birth to a boy, even the walls of the house rejoice. (Armenian)

In other parts of the world, people have also been taught to cry at the cradle of a daughter and cheer at the birth of a son. The disadvantages of a daughter are widely measured: she is 'a lost child' (Bengali), 'nobody's relative' (Mongo) and 'cigarettes' ashes' (Arabic).[273] The following statements are still popular in the Arab world:

> When a daughter is born, the threshold weeps for
>   forty days.
> Every daughter is a handful of trouble.
> Let's pray to the Prophet until the boy comes.

---

273   For details: *Never Marry a Woman with Big Feet*, Chapter 2: 93ff.

In various traditions, fathers still experience the birth of a girl as a shameful loss of face to other men in their own community. In Asia, female babies are often commented upon in extremely negative ways, for example, in China:

> Rather one son with a hump than eighteen golden
>   daughters.
> A stupid son is better than a crafty daughter.
> It is a blessing to bear a son, a calamity to bear a
>   daughter.

Or in India:

> Virtuous is the girl who suffers and dies without a
> sound. (Bengali)

> Those who lie, give birth to daughters. (Telugu)

> When a girl is born, don't take care of her, she will grow
> like a cactus; when a boy is born, take good care of him,
> as you would with a rose tree. (Rajasthani)

The latter proverb reflects a mentality that is common in many other Indian states, especially in the conservative north where many people have little or no school education and patriarchal culture is dominant. Of course, this is only the tip of a huge iceberg, only forcibly beginning to melt as the number of single young men who cannot find a wife has drawn attention to the increasing lack of girls.

What is the solution? Negative opinions about girls and daughters can change. In South Korea where the balance between the numbers of boys and girls was disturbed in the end of the twentieth and early twenty-first centuries, the government made a major effort to adjust social thinking patterns and cultural traditions. The situation there has now improved considerably. By questioning the preference for sons through paying attention to the problem in the media and in education, a new generation is growing up with a different mentality. Such government action shows that patient discussion about the origins and consequences of sexist traditions can turn the tables on patterns centuries old.[274]

Womb envy

Perfection in the form of androgyny must be a long-standing human wish, or there would not be so many stories in which our first ancestors were blessed with both sexes. Myths about world parents, in various iterations of bisexual unity, represent the universe as having a male and a female component. One example of a divine being with the characteristics of both human sexes is the Hindu god Brahma:

In the beginning, there was nothing but the Great Self, Brahman. That is to say, nothing but Brahman existed. […] Now Brahman looked around himself and saw nothing. He felt fear. […] Brahman was lonely [and] took the form of Brahma, the Creator. Brahma felt no delight; lonely people never do. He yearned for someone to keep him company and his thoughts split the temporary body he was using into two parts, like the halves of a clam shell coming apart. One of the two parts was male and the other female. They looked on

274 'Son Preference and Sex Ratio' infogram at www.womenstats.org.

each other as husband and wife. To this day, a happily married couple are like two parts of one being with Brahma in both of them.[275] (Hindu, India)

My neighbour in Lubumbashi, the Congolese writer and scholar Clémentine Faïk Nzuji, told me another story about the human loss of bisexual perfection. In Luba culture the first ancestor, Mvidi Mukulu, is 'a great hermaphrodite being' and lived happily in a beautiful garden. There was a wonderful palm tree in a light, open space in the middle of the garden. Only one thing was not permitted in the garden: you were not allowed to walk in a circle around the shady palm tree. A complete circle around the tree would disturb the perfect harmony in the garden. This ban led to an obsession:

> Our perfectly happy first ancestor wanted just one thing: to walk full circle around the palm tree, and one day this first human being began to walk around the motionless tree. Arrived at the starting point again, our ancestor fell apart in two halves. One half became man, the other half became woman. Ever since that time, men and women have been longing for the lost unity, a paradise they sometimes find briefly back in one another. (Luba, DR Congo)

Allegedly, it is thanks to that primal experience of completeness that men and women today feel attracted to one another.

In Plato's *Symposium*, written around 385 BCE, the conversation at a dinner party is devoted to the topic of bisexuality. The

---

275   This old myth originates from the *Brihadaranyaka Upanishad*, probably dating back to about 1500 BCE; the quoted passage is from *Parallel Myths*, 1994 pp. 39–40.

speaker explains that men and women keep looking for their lost perfection, which manifests itself in love and attraction between those of the same and different sexes. Here, ideal love either bridges the gap between a man and a woman or between people of the same sex.

Although almost every society is inclined to force children's hormonal processes in the direction of one sex or the other, in times of crisis, cultures often appeal to rituals in which men dress or behave like women or vice versa. This stems from a belief that male and female potencies, when combined in one person, will increase society's life force. To get access to that power, elements of both sexes are ritually brought together in one person – such as putting male seed on female breasts, rubbing menstrual blood onto young boys, or someone of the opposite sex eating a cut clitoris. It is thought that androgynous powers generate extra vitality.[276]

During times of calm, as opposed to coming together in one androgenous sex as in times of crisis, initiation rituals serve to clarify the differences between sexes. Rituals to turn boys into men are often more extensive than initiation rituals for girls, whose menstrual periods visibly mark the beginning of adolescence.

It is quite understandable that most researchers have paid less attention to male envy of women and female bodily functions than the other way around. Until well into the last century most anthropologists were men, and it is likely that they had a blind spot for male envy of women.[277] Yet that envy exists, and one of the most common devices to provide adolescents with a way of overriding it and to establish the required roles in society was to introduce initiation rites.

---

276 For a detailed study of androgyny, see Baumann.
277 See, for example, *Perceiving Women*, 1981.

The circumcision of boys exists in so many cultures around the world that it must meet a deep-seated need. Initiation rites sometimes serve as 'proof' that the men give birth to their sons without any female interference: the initiated boy is 'dying of his childhood' and is only now really born for the first time, thanks to his father.[278]

This form of wishful thinking puts medieval scholar Paolo da Certaldo's previously cited statement about the son who has to obey his father who gave birth to him[279], 'even though his mother provided practical aid' – in a wider context. It remains surprising that such reasonings have rarely been interpreted as womb envy. It looks as if, subconsciously, male envy led to ever stronger belief in the male seed as the essential contribution to the life of a child. The contribution of women in pregnancy and birth-giving was considered less important or even negligible.

Male initiation is almost everywhere more extensive than female and usually takes place during puberty, the period in which girls have their first monthly bleeding. It is not without significance that a little blood is released when the foreskin is cut away. In this process, female 'birthing behaviour' is sometimes literally imitated. Among the Iatmul in Papua New Guinea, boys even had a huge symbolic vulva thrown over their heads during their initiation. Emphasis on masculinity, (rebirth as a 'real man' or male birth-giving in circumcision rituals) frequently go along with explicit negative feelings towards women.[280]

During their initiation, boys, strongly influenced by their mothers and other women in the community in childhood,

---

278   Bettelheim, *Symbolic Wounds*: 104ff. Of course, jealousy is not the only motive for male initiation rites; they are also connected with fertility and the care for all the living.

279   Paolo da Certaldo (1320–70): 'A good son loves his father, has respect for him and obeys him, because he has given birth to him, even though his mother provided practical aid.'

280   Sierksma, Religie, *Sexualiteit en Agressie*, 1979 pp. 105 and 57; Bettelheim: 111ff.

receive the news that female influence and authority must no longer play a role in their lives. To be men, boys had to break free from the shackles of maternal care and learn not to be women.

Studying myths and other commentaries on the female body transmitted around the world, one cannot ignore the legacies brought forth by womb envy. They make understandable why men invented and imposed rules excluding women from religious and other professional practices. The usual explanation was (and in some traditions still is) that only men had the brains needed for those roles, for the very reason that they were men. Authors such as Françoise Héritier in her two-volume work *Masculin/Féminin* and Robert McElvaine in *Eve's Seed* argue the very opposite: those patterns of thinking ensue from what men were physically unable to do – giving birth to and suckling society's children.

In their practice, psychiatrists and psychotherapists come across men who are jealous of women. At children's dressing-up parties boys sometimes put pillows under their jerseys to imitate breasts or pregnant bellies. There are those who openly admit that they envy girls who will have children later: 'They hate them for it, and dream of violence; cutting off breasts, pulling out vaginas.' They feel frustrated by women not responding to their advances or simply for not being allowed to touch those breasts.[281] Freud continued to emphasise sexual differences and reaffirmed centuries of influential reasoning that women are 'inferior' to men. His emphasis on female penis envy and his claim that girls blame their mothers for having sent them 'so pathetically incomplete' into the world might well stem from his own subconscious womb envy.[282]

---

281 Oral information and literature, e.g. in Lederer pp. 55–56, 153; Bettelheim: 39ff.
282 McElvaine, Chapter 12.

The theft of women's secret

Why the male need for stories securing secrets and power from women, and why the long-standing tendency to exclude women from the public space? The argument in the Wulamba myth was that women had 'everything'. What they meant was that, in addition to their 'small penis', women had wombs producing all human offspring. That imbalance, experienced as a great injustice, had to be made up for by ruling out female performance in any other domain.

In many societies, power lies with those who have special knowledge or a secret society of members, who usually share a specific bond. During puberty rituals, youngsters become partakers of this secret knowledge for the first time. Among the Selknam in Tierra del Fuego, boys were even told during their initiation that they should never let their wives share in their intimate thoughts, 'for if you do, they might regain the power they had in the past.'[283]

A secret impresses as long as it remains hidden from outsiders. Stories say that 'once, long ago' women were in charge because they possessed a special secret, until the men managed to steal it from them. Since then, men have been in power and they will be for as long as they succeed in carefully guarding the secret among themselves and make sure it never falls back into the hands of women. No easy task, of course.

In some traditions, women are threatened with the belief that even accidentally seeing or touching the secret object(s) will make them drop dead immediately, or that knowing the secret or even having a vague conjecture about it is reason enough for them to be murdered. Usually, the secret takes the concrete form

---

283   Bierhorst p. 162.

of material objects such as ancestral masks, trumpets, flutes or bullroarers,[284] raffia skirts, wooden or stone artefacts with special powers, a ritual hut or sacred bags. According to the stories, originally such objects or power symbols were women's property; women had conceived, invented and made them.

Sometimes the secret is not even a tangible object, but consists of a ritual or of sacred songs. In some cases, the secret makes direct reference to the tyrannical power of women, cleverly overhauled by brave men after much male suffering, as we saw in the Gikuyu story from Kenya in which the men gained power by making all the women pregnant at the same time.

The Wulamba origin myth of the Australian Aboriginals tells of a similar theft in the Dreamtime, the time when the Djanggawul – the first ancestors – a brother and two sisters, were travelling together through the otherwise uninhabited land. On the way, lots of offspring constantly come forth from the wombs of the exceptionally fertile sisters, and it is the brother who takes care of laying these babies down on the grass: children born in each place are the first ancestors of the clans living there ever since.

No further news follows about female descendants, as the story focuses on a group of sons born from the wombs of the two sisters, joining their primal ancestor the Djanggawul brother. As men among each other, they complain about having 'nothing', not even symbols of their own, whereas the women have 'everything'. That is why they decide to take the *ngainmara* (folded mats representing the womb), containing the *rangga* (sacral poles, symbols of the penis). One day, in search of food, the two sisters leave these mighty symbols of their unstinting fertility

---

284 An ancient ritual wind instrument dating back to the Paleolithic period for communicating over great distances. It has been found in Europe, Asia, the Indian sub-continent, Africa, the Americas, and Australia: see Wikipedia, 'Bullroarer'.

and creativity unattended in the camp and the brother and his companions swoop in to steal them. When the women discover the theft, they run to the place where their brother is sitting with the other men. As soon as they see the women coming, the men begin to sing the sacred songs. Doing so, they prove that from now on, by stealing the fertility symbols, they have also taken from the sisters the authority to execute the sacred ritual that had been exclusively female. The younger sister anxiously wonders what to do now that they have lost their sacred symbols and power, but according to the older sister, this was not disastrous at all:

> We know everything. We have really lost nothing, for we remember it all, and we can let them have that small part. For aren't we still sacred, even if we have lost the bags? Haven't we still our uteri? And the younger Sister agreed with her.[285]

This comment reveals what it's all about: life-giving power. They certainly haven't lost it, but the symbolic theft marks an essential reversal in male/female relationships as well as in the division of labour. The men had always collected the food for the women and ground the nuts to knead bread. They had also taken care of the children, but from now on all this became women's work. Significantly, the reversal of roles was only possible due to the theft of the sacred power that from that point on belongs to the men. And there is more.

A crucial detail in the story is that the brother 'takes over' the bodies of the two sisters by considerably shortening their clitorises. Traditionally, the brother had an exceptionally long penis, while

---

285 This is a concise summary of the long and detailed Aboriginal story transcribed in Ronald M. Berndt, *Djanggawul: An Aboriginal Religious Cult of North-Eastern Arnhem Land*, 1952; the text is on pp. 40–41; the image on p. 25.

the sisters had no less spectacularly elongated clitorises. Like their brother with his penis, the sisters also left traces of their remarkable genitals in the sand wherever they walked.

From the moment the secret became the men's, their genitals radically change. The brother first cuts off the elder sister's clitoris until there is only a small piece left that does not extend beyond her thigh. Then he applies the same surgical intervention to the body of the younger sister:

> 'Ah,' said the Brother, 'Now you look more like proper women and it is easier for me to see the slit of your vulvae. Let me try them out.' First he copulated with the younger Sister. 'That feels nice,' he said. Then, turning to the elder Sister, he copulated with her too. 'That's very enjoyable,' he told her. 'I can feel the short end of the clitoris touching my penis, as I couldn't before.'[286]

The story does not report whether the women with their truncated clitorises appreciated or enjoyed the brother's performances. The brother argues that, from now on, the women have nothing to hide anymore and the man has free access to the vulva. Interestingly, the long clitorises cut off by the brother were the equivalent of and looked exactly like the poles (symbolising the phallus) in the sacred bags or mats, and are now lost forever to women. This robs the women of their 'masculinity' – according to the reasoning that a woman with a clitoris is a woman with a phallus. The Djanggawul brother still has his own long penis: en route he swings it over his shoulder and wraps it around his neck, just as before. The Wulamba story seems to confirm a new status quo, but appearances deceive, as fear has not been overcome:

---

286   *Ibid.*

In the myth the women catch fish by sitting in the
water with their legs spread apart and by catching their
victims in this unmistakable trap [...]. In daily life a
copulating woman is referred to as the one catching a
fish. A similar symbol is the whale, from whose mouth
a small fish barely escapes.

Such references are reminiscent of the frightful devouring mother
or the '*vagina dentata*'.[287]

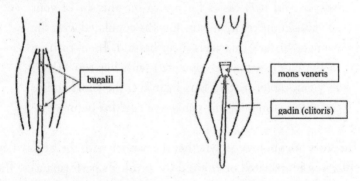

The impressive genitals of the Djanggawul brother and elder sister. Drawings by
Aboriginal informants, *c.* 1950.

During annual fertility festivals the Aboriginal men dance in a
circle to commemorate the symbolic reversal of power relations.
They bombard the *ngainmara* with their *rangga* while the women
and children wriggle for a while under the folded mats and
imitate unborn babies who, like all ancestors, emerge from the
fertile wombs of the Djanggawul sisters. The pole-wielding men
show that they are in charge of the fertility ritual, but Aboriginal
informers, men themselves, believe that women should actually

287   Sierksma 1979 p. 180. Translation is author's own.

lead the ritual: 'We still know that they are the real leaders,' because 'the men have stolen it all.'[288]

In addition to peoples such as the Wulamba and Aranda in Australia, the theme of stolen sacred objects also occurs in West Africa, Papua New Guinea and in Central and South America. The myths share common topics and ultimately the message below, summarised from South American myths:

> First, the sacred objects belonging to men (masks, trumpets, ritual lodges, songs, and the like) originally were invented by women and owned by them; or, if they originated with the men, their secrets were discovered by women, who contaminated their sacredness by viewing or touching them [...] Spying on the sacred instruments was a death warrant for all violators of the prohibition.

A second theme running through these myths is that a position of authority adheres to the possessors of tribal secrets, and that those who sit in authority, whether females or males, may also enjoy a life of relative leisure.

The trumpets and lodges are the badge of this authority, permitting one sex to dominate the other. However begun, the myths invariably conclude with the men in power. Either the men have taken from the women the symbols of authority and have installed themselves as the rightful owners of the ceremony and its paraphernalia, or they invoke violent sanctions against the women who have dared to challenge male authority. In no version do the women win the battle for power. Instead, they remain forever the subjects of male terrorism, hidden in their

---

288   See Berndt pp. 2–3 and 40.

huts, fearing to look out on masked spirits and trumpeting ancestors.[289]

In many cultures, children and women were instilled with paranoid fear, believing that the sight of these power symbols was deadly. Men who wear ancestor masks represent the powerful spirits of those ancestors. It is only at their initiation that boys are taught that these dancing spirits are ordinary men.

In his novel *Things Fall Apart*, the Nigerian writer Chinua Achebe refers to this traditional ritual in his own Igbo society, where the masked dancers are called *egwugwu*:

> The drums sounded again and a flute blew. The *egwugwu* house was now a pandemonium of quavering voices [filling] the air as the spirits of the ancestors, just emerged from the earth, greeted themselves in their esoteric language. The *egwugwu* house into which they emerged faced the Forest, away from the crowd [...]
>
> And then the *egwugwu* appeared. The women and children sent up a great shout and took to their heels. It was instinctive. A woman fled as soon as an *egwugwu* came in sight. And when, as on that day, nine of the greatest masked spirits in the clan came out together. It was a terrifying spectacle.[290]

Sometimes the men's protection of their secret knowledge against female outsiders takes excessive forms. In *Le Cru et le Cuit*, Lévi-Strauss describes a horrific Chamacoco story (Paraguay/Brazil) in which, unexpectedly, the secret of the mask-wearing men falls back into the hands of women. The Chamacoco woman who

---

289 Bamberger quoted in Weigle p. 281.
290 Achebe pp. 62–63.

finds out the mighty secret is a mother who had shortly before been raped by her own son:

> A young man was laying sick in his hammock when he briefly saw his mother's vulva. She had climbed the roof of the cabin to fix the covering. Desire flashing into him, he waited until she came down again and raped her.[291]

Right after the rape, the son has a moment of weakness that the mother aptly makes use of by stealing the secret of the masks – knowledge taboo to women, and meant to be told among men only: 'Since the myth itself contained the secret of the masks, to share it with the opposite sex would have endangered the male-dominated society that men evidently felt to be always on the brink of collapse.'[292]

As soon as the men realise that this mother knows their secret and has also shared it with the other women, they are so deeply shocked that there seems to be no other solution than to kill all women. One woman succeeds in escaping the slaughter, but that is, of course, not the end of the story.

One day, the only surviving woman attracts the attention of a man walking under the tree in which she's hiding. The man gets such an erection that he is unable to climb up to her and the other men rushing in fail as well. Eventually, they catch the woman, rape her and cut her into pieces that end up soaked in sperm under the tree. All the men choose a piece of that seed-soaked flesh and take it back to the village, each of them puts it inside his own home. Then they leave again to go fishing together.

---

291 In Lévi-Strauss, Le Cru et le Cuit, 1964 p. 120.
292 Bierhorst, 2002 p. 137.

On their return, they find that a complete woman has sprouted from each body part of the murdered and sliced-up woman – the breasts, abdomen and thighs have turned into fat women, while the thin ones remind us that they had once been fingers and toes.

This is how new life originated from the last surviving life-producing woman even after she had been killed, the only one left who knew the men's secret and thereby caused terrifying panic. The story is directly inspired by and connected with the oldest agriculture. A multitude of new lives is being created by cutting up the dead body into pieces, in exactly the same way as women divided their tubers and tucked them into the ground to grow new crops.

Hunting is older than agriculture, and the usual division of labour was that men hunted and women gathered food. The first steps towards growing crops were something unprecedented. The discovery that by sowing seeds close to home, placing banana cuttings and tubers into the ground, you can grow new banana trees and yield new tubers, was a real milestone in cultural history. Sierksma and others consider agriculture as women's invention. Or, in the words of an Indian informant in the Orinoco area: 'The women who give birth to the children also know best how the plants can be multiplied.'[293]

As men often returned from the hunt empty-handed, the women took care of the larger share of the food supply via the proceeds from their own piece of land, and relationships between the sexes changed:

> The invention of agriculture meant the emancipation of
> women, and men in these old equatorial cultures found
> it as difficult to cope with as their twentieth-century

---

[293] Sierksma, 1962 p. 144.

peers. Hence, in areas around the equator, agriculture began to become more important than hunting, and men sometimes resented women who had crushed their sense of indispensability.[294]

Hunters who had felt superior as breadwinners in households and communities that until then had depended solely or mainly on them, must have experienced the food input of women as threatening. This led to the establishment of male-only secret societies as a psychologically indispensable counter-offensive to restore superiority. With a prestigious secret, the men could renew their assumed right to authority and all the privileges derived from it, enabling them to get women and children to do unpleasant work for them.

A Chukchi myth clearly manifests male unease about the inequality of creation capacity. The male creator, Raven, sees his wife first swell and then give birth to two children she calls people, and she seems intensely satisfied in a strange way. Her life-giving activity upsets him so much he feels a deep urge to create something himself, all the more since his wife presses him to produce a place on which their children can live. Raven gravely doubts he will be able to do so and the children laugh at him. In the end he solves his problem by shitting and peeing with all his might until his body is completely wasted. And that's how mountains and valleys, rivers, oceans, and lakes came into being – a world fit for the first humans.[295]

Wouldn't life have been a lot more manageable for a man if he were in control of all reproduction? All kinds of stories ponder this – often between the lines – but some writers openly admit

---

294 *Ibid.* p. 145.
295 In his essay, 'Earth Diver: Creation of the Mythopoeic Male', Alan Dundes refers to the ideas of Erich Fromm and other psychoanalysts, 1980 p. 279.

this need for control. In ancient Greek philosophy, the idea of the innate inferiority of women was so common that the Greek poet and thinker Hesiod (mid eighth century BCE) called the 'race of women … an evil to mortal men, with a nature to do evil.' He found it extremely regrettable that a man could not reproduce his own kind without a woman's intervention.[296]

The fact that women give birth to sons and daughters can be read as a variation on the principle identified by historian Jan Romein as an 'inhibiting lead'.[297] Female ownership of procreation encouraged men to go beyond birth-giving capacity in as many other areas as possible – economics, politics, science, art and culture, to name a few. Exclusion of women in all these areas has been perpetuated through the ages. Partly thanks to the unwavering cement of myths, a world order was created that raised one gender above the other out of an immense need for compensation.

296   Hesiod 7–9 and Semonides in Lloyd/Jones, Hugh. *Females of the Species*, 1975:18ff.
297   Jan Romein in *De dialektiek van de vooruitgang*, 1937 pp. 9–64.

A FINAL NOTE

SOONER OR LATER in global stories, men succeeded in stealing women's secrets. By retelling the myth that there was chaos before men were in charge, existing patriarchal dominance has been confirmed over and over again. Many myths magnify the differences between the sexes and invented rules in which all tasks were divided hierarchically by gender, age, race and class. Those who want to keep the birth-giving privilege in check apply two mechanisms: on the one hand, belittling the female mind and body; on the other hand, warning against destructive female power.

Through the myths that have been passed down through generations, we have seen a wealth of appropriation of the female body, and a rich early history where female body worship was prevalent. We have also seen the male envy of female body parts – chiefly the breasts and womb, on account of their life-giving abilities. If stories about male creators, male divine breasts and pregnancies represent male birth-giving and breastfeeding wishes, then the fulfilment of those wishes is getting closer.

Breastfeeding fatherhood promises a new balance, the beginning of the end of the ancient injustices. It also promises further disruption: in May 2016, a flash mob of young men in China appeared on Mother's Day, clasping fake babies to their bare male breasts. The stunt was received with varying degrees of support.

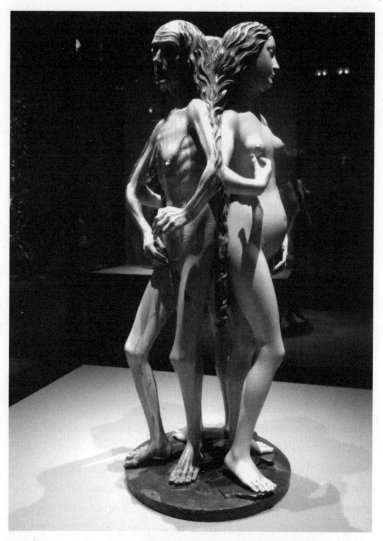

Allegory of Vanity by Michel Erhart or Jörg Syrlin the Elder. Lime wood, Ulm, Kunsthistorisches Museum, Vienna, *c.* 1470–1480.

Suit Supply 'Toy Boys'
advertising poster at a tram stop
in Amsterdam, 2016.

Physiologist and evolutionary biologist Jared Diamond predicted
in the 1990s that the human species would indeed be 'a leading
candidate for male lactation', because in combination with
hormonal injections, manual stimulation of a father's nipples
will stimulate the dormant but present potential to produce
milk.[298] Soon, with the help of science, men, women and those
who identify as non-binary and intersex – as well as transgender
people who are both male and female presenting – really could
share all birth-giving, breastfeeding and other care duties. As
humans we are growing closer to one another and resembling
each other more than ever.

The fears men have of women and their body power, told in
contemporary psychiatric sessions, are surprisingly similar to
events referred to in ancient myths and stories. The heavy stone

---

298   Jared Diamond quoted in Richter, pp.8–9.

of the mythical past still weighs down on the back of the present. The projection of destructive urges onto the opposite sex turns women into monsters or witches celebrating their gruesome lust at the cost of men's wellbeing, while in reality, the reverse occurs far more often.

Throughout history, rulers large and small have considered the bodies and labour of their subjects to be at their disposal. They do not think of those belonging to the underlying groups – be that gender, age, race or class-driven – as fellow humans. In his book *The Power Paradox* (2017), American psychologist Dacher Keltner argues that power makes people less empathetic. In an interview with a newspaper in the Netherlands, he cited the behaviour of Donald Trump as an example: 'His focus is primarily on maintaining power. He makes impulsive decisions, disrespectful comments and tells self-glorifying stories – all signs of abuse of power, which evoke stress and anxiety in others. Stress is a pre-eminent characteristic of powerlessness.'[299] Power has to be handled with care. The one who has more power – physically, sexually, financially, intellectually – has more responsibility for adopting humane conduct, a golden rule that holds for all human beings.

Several scholars explain aggression and dominance among men as a reaction to male awareness of female body power. The institutional arrangements that embody male dominance and the cultural justification of it are confirmed by creation and origin myths, and also by the many contemptuous proverbs about threatening female power and popular culture in general. Of course, the impact of continuous negative messages over the centuries has been enormous. Their echoes still resound all over the world and a majority of contemporary women still believe that a woman is unfit for a leadership position.

---

299 NRC-Handelsblad, December 2017, pp.9–10.

In the past women have often been made to believe that their bodies were not theirs, while men were told that a woman's body was meant to have a male owner. Economic dependence led women to present their bodies as seductively as possible, because without the opportunity to develop themselves professionally, the body was their only capital in life. The role of passive, beautiful object has been fed to women for centuries and still holds its power thanks to merciless advertisers. The images, ideals and ideas imposed on women today encourage female submissiveness no less than binding religious laws and cultural codes of conduct have always done. An ongoing struggle is needed not to submit.

It has never been easy to overcome resistance and practise autonomy, especially for those who have internalised their submissive position. Women must get rid of their perceived 'traditional' role as a silently pleasing object and claim freedom that is rooted in qualities and talents, qualities that have nothing to do with body parts or their appearance. Male fear and awe still exist everywhere, but women are too little aware of their power.

Under the thin layer of contemporary society's asphalt lie the well-preserved and well-entrenched ideas of our ancestors. A search for handed-down views about body parts unique to women not only yields knowledge about past conceptions, but also valuable insights into the changing position of so many women, which has caused confusion on multiple fronts. We cannot change history, but we can alter our way of looking at the past and how we approach the present.

If we are to think of the different genders as circles orbiting one another in a venn diagram, the more overlap we have, and the more awareness of what we share, the more able we are to talk with one another. If we cannot speak to those not in our circle, how can we progress? The body, after all, is 'not so black and white', with a wink to Kenan Malik's book. There are multiple variants, but the great similarities between men, women, intersex, non-binary and trans people have historically been ignored, because the emphasis on the differences between genders kept the hierarchy intact. I look forward to reading the future works about the experience of trans individuals and how their experience of body parts resonates and differs from the experiences of cisgendered individuals. There should be space on our shelves and in our minds for a rich diversity of collective heritage and lived experiences. However, unyielding positions on identity politics have got, and continue to get, in the way of engaging in open dialogue with each other.

Our common and vulnerable human values as formulated in the UN Human Rights Charter give hope and pave the way towards steady progress in social justice, and respect for equal human rights. All those who are not in our group are not necessarily our enemy.

People have always been able to adjust ingrained patterns of life, challenge themselves and each other, and take new trajectories. Instead of a fixation on phallus or vagina monologues, why not explore dialogues about how people can do better together, with an eye on each other's vulnerabilities and collective celebration of one another's strengths.

ACKNOWLEDGEMENTS

I am grateful to Hedda Post, Els Rutten and Reimar Schefold, close friends and colleagues, for stimulating conversation and commentary during the writing of this book and for reading earlier parts of the text. Others patiently shared their specialised knowledge or a relevant illustration: Wim Boot, Matthi Forrer, Theo Krispijn, Lily van der Stokker, Yvo Smit and Joop de Vries.

I owe a great deal to several Leiden University librarians for outstanding service, especially Arnoud Vrolijk, Jef Schaeps, Karin Schepers and Kasper van Ommen, and I owe special thanks to Erik Geleijns, conservator of the Medieval Collections at both the Royal Library and The House of the Book in The Hague. The Wellcome Trust in London generously made their special collections available in the public domain, which I used for research. Some of the artwork has made its way into this book. My thanks also to my editor at The Westbourne Press, Elizabeth Briggs, for overall interest, unflagging enthusiasm, patience and helpful suggestions. Last but not least: thank you, Laura Susijn (and the Susijn Agency in London), for your acumen, continuing support and lasting friendship.

PERMISSIONS

The following photographers and owners kindly gave their permission for the photographs, texts and works of art found on these pages:

xiv Leiden University Libraries; **16** Archeological Museum Athens; **18** Left: Blaubeuren Museum of Prehistory, Germany; right: Museum of Natural History, Vienna, Austria; **21** Museo del Prado, Madrid; **24** National Anthropological Museum, Mexico City; **27** Xinjiang Uighur Autonomous Region Museum, Xinjiang, China; **32** Museum of Anatolian Civilizations, Ankara, Turkey; **39** Photo: Joop de Vries; **46** Woodcut by South-African artist Motshile wa Nthodi, 1979. Taken from 'The Black Paradise', a collection of African origin myths revised by Mineke Schipper (1980); **52** Musée du Louvre, Paris; **55** Eretz Israel Museum, Tel Aviv. Photo: Ashtoret Anat; **63** Lessines, Museum Hôpital Notre-Dame à la Rose, Belgium. Photo: Francis Vauban, with many thanks to Elise Boquet, conservator; **64** *Encyclopaedia Biblica*, 1903; **66** Grand Curtius Museum, Liege; **70** Wellcome Collection, London; **72** left: Musée des Arts Décoratifs, Paris; right: German National Museum, Neurenberg. Photo: Wolfgang Sauber; **75** Museum of Natural History, Vienna; **77** left: Royal Museum of Fine Arts, Antwerp; right: anonymous copy of an older painting (possibly by Jean Fouquet), Chateau de Loches; **80**

Leiden University Libraries; **84** upper: Indonesian fertility jewellery, Flores Island (author's own collection); lower left: Archeological Museum Athens; lower right: Wellcome Collection, London; **89** The Michael Rockefeller Memorial Collection; **92** Archeological Museum Athens; **94** Musée du Louvre, Paris; Archeological Museum Athens; **95** Wikimedia Commons; **98** Honolulu Museum of Art; **99** State Art Collections of Dresden, AKG-Images; **109** womanstats.org, 2015; **112** Larco Erotica Museum, Lima. Photo: Pfrishauf; **118** Bibliothèque Nationale de France; **120** Afrika Museum, Berg en Dal; **143** Musée du Louvre, Paris: Fould Collection; **150** Antoni van Leeuwenhoek, *Epistolae*, 1719, p. 156; **156** Wellcome Collection, London; **158** Wellcome Collection, London; **161** Capitoline Museums, Rome. Photo: Jastrow; **166** Leiden University Libraries; **170** Wellcome Collection, London; **172** Frans Halsmuseum, Haarlem; **174** Roman copy of a Hellenistic original. Capitoline Museums, Rome; **177** Museum Valckhof, Nijmegen. Photo: Joop de Vries; **179** Leiden University Libraries; **180** Musée des Civilisations de l'Europe et de la Mediterranée, Marseille; **191** Museum of Printing and Graphic Communication, Lyon; **192** 'Breasts' by Frieda Hughes is published in the collection *Out of the Ashes* (Bloodaxe Books, 2018) by Frieda Hughes and is reprinted here by kind permission of Bloodaxe Books; **192** https://www.weirdasianews.com/2006/12/07/japanese-breast-pudding-yummy/, 2017; **198** Church of the Holy Selpulchre, Barletta; **200** Royal Library, The Hague. Medieval manuscript KB 76f2, 278r_min.; **205** right: National Archeological Museum, Athens; **207** Walters Art Museum, Baltimore, Maryland; **212** *Plos and Bartels*, p. 127; **213** photo: Stefano Mortello, Catania; **214** left: Foltermuseum, Freiburg, photo: I. Stöcklin; right: Fortress Museum, Salzburg. Photo: Klaus D. Peter; **216** Leiden University Libraries; **219** womanstats. org, 2014; **228** Leiden University Libraries; **232** left: Mario Karbel, Alma Mater Havana; right: John Legate, Alma Mater Camtabrigia; **244** University College, London; **252** Kunsthistorisches Museum, Vienna.

BIBLIOGRAPHY

Achebe, Chinua, *Things Fall Apart*, Penguin Classics, 1958.

Addington Symonds, John, *Wine, Women, and Song: Medieval Latin Students' Songs*, Chatto & Windus, 1840.

Amahazion F, 'Breast ironing: A brief overview of an underreported harmful practice,' *Journal of global health*, *11*, 03055.

Angier, Nathalie, *Woman: An Intimate Geography*, Mariner Books, 1999.

Anon. '500 Years of Virgin Mary Sightings in One Map', *National Geographic*, 13 November 2015.

Anon. 'Claridge's breastfeeding row: Protest by mothers', *BBC News*, 6 December 2014.

Anon. 'Does God Have Breasts?', *The Queen of Heaven Wordpress*, 2011.

Aristotle, *On the Generation of Animals Book Four*, translation from the Greek: eBooks University of Adelaide, Australia.

Ardener, Edwin, *Perceiving Women*, ed. Shirley Ardener, Malaby Press, 1977.

Armstrong, Karen, *A Short History of Myth*, Canongate, 2005.

Athanassakis, Apostolos N., *Orphic Hymns: Text and Translation*, Johns Hopkins University Press, 2013.

Atlantico Magazine, 'Japon prendrez biern verre lait maternel', 26 May 2015.

Bahrani, Zainab, *Women of Babylon: Gender and Representation in Mesopotamia*, Routledge, 2001.

Baring, Anne and Cashford, Jules, *The Myth of the Goddess: Evolution of an Image*, Penguin, 1993.

Baumann, Hermann, *About Androgyny Worldwide*, Das doppelte Geschlecht, 1955.

Bekers, Elisabeth, *Dissecting Anthills of W/Human Insurrection: A Comparative Study of African Creative Writing on Female Genital Excision*, University of Antwerp, 2002.

Bettelheim, Bruno, *Symbolic Wounds*, The Free Press, 1954.

Berndt, Ronald M., *Djanggawul: An Aboriginal Religious Cult of North-Eastern Arnhem Land*, Routledge, 2004, 1952.

Bierhorst, John, *The Mythology of South America*, Oxford University Press, 2002.

Boas, Franz; Alexander Teit, James; Farrand, Livingston; Gould, Marian K.; Spinden, Herbert Joseph. *Folk-tales of Salishan and Sahaptin Tribes*, American Folklore Society, 1969.

Bogoras, Waldemar, *Chukchee Mythology*, Forgotten Books, 2007.

Branigan, Tania, Vidal, John, 'Hands up or we strip!', *The Guardian*, 22 July 2002.

Brulliard, Karin, 'Why Goats Used to Breastfeed Human Babies', *Washington Post*, 25 February 2016.

Al-Bukhari, Muhammad, *Sahih al-Bukhari* Arabic-English translation, Vol. VII.

Calisch, I.M, Calisch N.S, *Nieuw woordenboek der Nederlandsche taal*, 1864 .

Crawley, Ernest, *The Mystic Rose: A Study of Primitive Marriage*, Spring Books, 1902.

Dashu, Max, 'Xi Wangmu, The shamanic great goddess of China',

Supressed Histories Archive.

De Clercq and Schmelz, T, Ethnographische beschrijving van de West-en Noordkust van Nederlandsch Nieuw Guinea. Trap, 1893.

Del Rei, Arundel, *Creation Myths of the Formosan Natives.* The Hokuseido Press, 1951.

Delaney, Carol, 'Mortal Flow: Menstruation in Turkish Village Society' in Blood Magic (ed. Buckley and Gottlieb), University of California Press, 1988.

Dempwolff, Otto, 'Märchen der Zalamo und Hehe in Deutsch Ost-Afrika,' *Anthropophyteia*, 1904.

Dikehowa, Precious, 'Should Men Stay off Wives' Breasts?', *The Nation*, 23 October 2015.

Doniger O'Flaherty, Wendy, *Women, Androgynes and Other Mythical Beasts*, Chicago University Press, 1980.

Dor, Juliette, 'The Sheela-na-Gig: An Incongruous Sign of Sexual Purity', *Medieval Virginities* (ed. Bernau, Evans and Salih), 2003.

Drewal, Henry, 'Efe: Voiced Power and Pageantry', *African Arts* 7 (2), 1974.

Dundes, Alan, 'Earth-Diver: Creation of the Mythopoeic Male.' *American Anthropologist* 64, no. 5, 1962.

Ebeling, Erich, *Quellen zur Kenntnis der Babylonischen Religion*, Leipzig, 1918.

Eco, Umberto, *A History of Ugliness*, Harvill Secker, 2007.

Eisenmenger, *Natursagen*, 1711, 1907.

Eliade, Mircea, *Myths, Dreams and Mysteries*, Harper Collins, 1979.

Ellis, A.B., *The Yoruba-speaking Peoples*, Routledge, 1894.

Elwin, Verrier, 'The Vagina Dentata Legend', *British Journal of Medical Psychology*, 1943.

Elwin, Verrier, *Myths of the North-East Frontier of India*, Gyan Publishing, 1958.

Elwin, Verrier, *Myths of Middle India*, Oxford University Press India, 1949.

Englard, Yaffa, 'The Creation of Eve in Art and the Myth of Androgynous Adam', *Ars Judaica* (5) 2009.

Erdoes, Richard and Ortiz, Alfonso, *American Indian Myths and Legends*, Pantheon, 1984.

Evans-Pritchard, E.E., 'Some Collective Expressions of Obscenity in Africa,' *The Journal of the Royal Anthropological Institute*, 1929.

Faye Koren, Sharon, *Forsaken: The Menstruant in Medieval Jewish Mysticism*, Brandeis University Press, 2011.

Feng, Gia-fu and English, Jane, *Tao Te-Ching*, Vintage Books, 1972.

Fromm, Erich, *The Forgotten Language*, Atlantic Books, 2000.

Ginzberg, Louis, *The Legends of the Jews*, Philadelphia, 1969.

Graves, Robert and Patai, Raphael, *Hebrew Myths: The Book of Genesis*, Anchor Books/Doubleday, 1964.

Griaule, Marcel, *Dieu d'Eau*, Fayard, 1966.

Groskop, Viv, 'Not Your Mother's Milk', *Guardian Health*, 5 January 2007.

Hadland Davis, F., *Myths and Legends of Japan*, Dover Publications, 1914.

Hall, Amy, 'Cameroon's Women Call Time on Breast Ironing', *New Internationalist*, 1 May 2013.

Héritier, Françoise. *Masculin/Féminin II: Dissoudre la Hiérarchie*, Editions Odile Jacob, 2002.

Hesiod, *Theogony*, OUP Oxford, 2008.

Hinsch, Bret, 'Prehistoric Images of Women from the North China Region: The Origins of Chinese Goddess Worship?' *Journal of Chinese Religions, 31.1*, 2004.

Hogbin, Ian, *The Island of Menstruating Men*, Chandler Publishing, 1970.

Hollander, Anne, *Seeing Through Clothes*, University of California

Press, 1978.

Hufton, Olwen, *The Prospect Before Her: A History of Women in Western Europe 1500–1800*, Vintage, 1998.

Hughes, Frieda, 'Breasts', from the collection *Out of the Ashes*, Bloodaxe Books, 2001.

Huixin, Zhou, 'Filial Piety Touches Heaven: stories of virtuous daughters-in-law', The Epoch Times, 29 April, 2016.

Idema, Wilt, 'Bespied in bad', *De Boekenwereld*, 2017.

Islam Web, 'Wet-nurses of Prophet Muhammad', 5 January 2012.

Jacobsen, Thorkild, *The Harps That Once ... Sumerian Poetry in Translation*, Yale University Press, 1987.

Jahn, Janheinz, 'Black Orpheus, A Journal of African and Afro-American Literature', Vol. II, January 1958.

Kim, Monica, 'Is it socially acceptable to breastfeed in public?', *Vogue*, 10 May 2016.

Ke, Yuan, *Dragons and Dynasties: An Introduction to Chinese Mythology*, Penguin Books, 1993.

Keuls, Eva C., *The Reign of the Phallus*, University of California Press, 1985.

Knight, Mary, 'Curing cut or ritual mutilation? Some remarks on the practice of female and male circumcision in Graeco-Roman Egypt.' *Isis; an international review devoted to the history of science and its cultural influences* vol. 92,2, 2001.

Kuo, Lily, 'In China, wealthy adults drink breast milk while millions of infants stick with formula', *Quartz*, 15 July 2023.

Wilson, J.R., 'Ethnological Notes on the Kwottos of Toto (Panda) District, Keffi Division, Benue Province, Northern Nigeria,' *Journal of the African Society* XXXVII, 1927–1928.

Laqueur, Thomas, *Making Sex: Body and Gender from the Greeks to Freud*, Harvard University Press, 1990.

Lawrence, Denise L., 'Menstrual Politics: Women and Pigs in Rural

Society,' *Blood Magic*, University of California Press, 2010.

Lederer, Wolfgang, *Fear of Women*, Grune & Stratton, 1968.

Leeming, David, *Myth. A Biography of Belief*, Oxford University Press, 2003.

Lerner, Geda, *The Creation of Patriarchy*, Oxford University Press, 1987.

Lévi-Strauss, Claude, *Le Cru et le Cuit*, Plon, 1964.

Lihui Yang and Deming An, *Handbook of Chinese Mythology*, ABC-CLIO, 2005.

Lowie, Robert H., *Primitive Religion*, Liveright Publishing, 1925.

Geller, Markham; Schipper, Mineke, *Imagining Creation*, Brill, 2007.

Ginzberg, Louis, *The Legends of the Jews*. Trans. Henrietta Szold. Seven vols. Vol. I:65. 1967– 1969.

Mackie, Gerry, 'Ending Footbinding and Infibulation: A Convention Account,' *American Sociological Review* 61 (6), December 1996.

Malik, Kenan, *Not So Black and White: A History of Race from White Supremacy to Identity Politics*, Hurst, 2003.

Martin, Emily, in *Woman: An Intimate Geography*, Virago 1999.

Mathieu, Rémi, *Étude sur la mythologie et l'ethnologie de la Chine ancienne, Traduction annotée du Shanhai jing*, Collège de France, Institut des Hautes Éudes Chinoises, 1983.

McElvaine, Robert, *Eve's Seed*, McGraw-Hill Education, 2001.

Meshel, Ze'ev, 'Kuntillet 'Ajrud. An Israelite Religious Center in Northern Sinai,' *Expedition 20*, 1978.

Miftahi, Mufti Zaferruddin, *Modesty and Chastity in Islam*, Qazi Publishers, 1993.

Miles, Margaret R., *A Complex Delight*, University of California Press, 2008.

Miller, Geoffrey, *The Mating Mind*, Vintage Books, 2001.

Mozzani, Eloïse, *Le Livre des Superstitions: Mythes, Croyances et Légendes*, Robert Laffont, 1995.

Munroe, Ruth H., Carol, Robert L., Ember, Melvin, 'The Conditions Favoring Matrilocal Versus Patrilocal Residence,' *American Anthropologist* 73, 1971.

Noah Harari, Yuval, *Sapiens*, Harper, 2011.

NRC newspaper, back page 'Van kut naar superkut', NRC Handelsblad, 27 February 2017.

Ogundipe, Sola and Obinna, Chioma, 'Exclusive breast feeding: Whither Nigeria in the campaign', *Vanguard*, 7 August 2011.

O'Rourke, P.F., 'The Wt-Woman,' *Zeitschrift für Ägyptische Sprache und Altertumskunde*, Vol. 134, 2, 2007.

Oosthoek, Nathan, 'NOVUM questionnaire met Andreas Kinneging,' *NOVUM*, 9 April 2018.

Osborn, M.S., 'The Rent Breasts: A Brief History of Wet-nursing,' *Midwife, Health Visitor & Community Nurse*, 1979; 15(8).

P–L. Couchoud, 'Le mythe de la danseuse obscène,' *Mercure de France*, July–August 1929.

Pagels, Elaine, 'What Became of God the Mother? Conflicting Images of God in Early Christianity,' *Signs* (2) 1976.

Pagels, Elaine, *The Gnostic Gospels*, Vintage Books, 1979.

Paley, Maggie, *The Book of the Penis*, Grove Press, 1999.

Papyrus Bremner-Rind 26, 21–27, *1 Bibliotheca Aegyptica* 3, Brussels 1933.

Patai, Raphael, *The Hebrew Goddess*, Wayne State University Press, 1968.

Paulme, Denise, 'La mère dévorante', *Journal des Africanistes*, 1975.

Ploss, Hermann and Bartels, Max, *De Vrouw in Natuur – en Volkenkunde Anthropologische Studiën*, Clgveldt Amsterdam 1912.

Prior, Mary, *Women in English Society*, 1500–1800, Routledge, 1991.

Radbill, Samuel X., 'The Role of Animals in Infant Feeding' in *Wayland D. Hand, American Folk Medicine: A Symposium*. University of California Press, 1976.

Rahmouni, Aicha, *Storytelling in Chefchaouen Northern Morocco*, Brill, 2014.

Ranke-Heinemann, Uta, *Eunuchs for the Kingdom of God: Women, Sexuality, and the Catholic Church*, Doubleday, 1990.

Rasmussen, Knud, *Intellectual Culture of the Iglulik Eskimos*, Forgotten Books, 1976.

Reeves Sanday, Peggy, *Female Power and Male Dominance: On the Origin of Sexual Inequality*, Cambridge University Press, 1988.

Rogers, Lois, 'Earth Dads Give Breast Milk a Try', *The Sunday Times*, 13 March 2005.

Rodriguez, Sarah W., 'Rethinking the History of Female Circumcision and Clitoridectomy: American Medicine and Female Sexuality in the Late Nineteenth Century,' *Journal of the History of Medicine and Allied Sciences*, 63 (3), July 2008.

Sabbah, Fatna A. (Fatima Mernissi), *Woman in the Muslim Unconscious*, Pergamon Press, 1984.

Saintyves, P. *Les vierges mères*, Forgotten Books, 1908.

Saner, Emine, 'Brace yourself for the Mother of All Cheeses' *The Guardian*, 9 March.

Satlow, Michael L., 'Jewish Constructions of Nakedness', *Journal of Biblical Literature*, 1997.

Saxon, Elizabeth, *The Eucharist in Romanesque France: Iconography and Theology*, Boydell Press, 2006.

Schafer, Edward H., 'Ritual Exposure in Ancient China', *Harvard Journal of Asiatic Studies Vol. 14*, No. 1/2, 1951.

Schipper, Mineke, *Never Marry a Woman with Big Feet* Speaking Tiger, 2004

Schipper, Mineke, *In the Beginning There Was No One*, Prometheus, 2010.

Shaikh, Ulfat and Ahmed, Omar 'Islam and Infant Feeding,' *Breastfeeding Medicine*, I.3, 2006.

Shaw, Teresa, *The Burden of the Flesh*, Augsburg Fortress Publishers, 1998.

Sierksma, Rypke *Religie, Sexualiteit en Agressie,* Uitgeverij Konstapel, 1979.

Sierksma, Fokke, *De roof van het vrouwengeheim*, Mouton & Co, 1962.

Silverman, Eric K., 'Anthropology and Circumcision,' *Annual Review of Anthropology*, 2004.

Smith, Merril D., *Cultural Encyclopedia of the Breast*, Rowman and Littlefield Publishers, 2014.

Srinivasan, Doris Meth, *Many Heads, Arms and Eyes*, Brill, 1997.

Steenbrink, Karel, *Adam Redivivus: Muslim elaborations of the Adam Saga with special reference to the Indonesian literary traditions*, Meinema-Zoetermeer, 1998.

Stol, Marten, *Women in the Ancient Near East,* De Gruyter, 2016.

Ting-jui, Ho, *A Comparative Study of Myths and Legends from Formosan Aborigines*, unpublished thesis, Indiana University, 1967.

Torday, E. and Joyce, T.A., *Notes Ethnographiques*, Falk Fils, 1910.

van Gulik, R.H. *Sexual Life in Ancient China*, Brill, 2021.

Walker Bynum, Caroline, *Jesus as Mother: Studies in the Spirituality of the High Middle Ages*, University of California Press, 1984.

Waterfield, Gordon, *Sultans of Aden*, John Murray, London 1968.

Weigle, Marta, *Creation and Procreation*, University of Pennsylvania Press, 1989.

Weigle, Marta, *Spiders & Spinsters: Women and Mythology*, University of New Mexico Press, 1982.

Wettlaufer, Jürgen, 'The *jus primae noctis* as a male power display: A review of historic sources with evolutionary interpretation', *Evolution and Human Behaviour*, 21 vol 2, 2000.

Withuis, Jolande, 'Mannen hebben de komst van vrouwen in hun domein nog niet verwerkt', *Trouw*, 25 November 2017.

Wolfe, Barnard, *The Daily Life of a Chinese Courtesan Climbing up a Tricky Ladder: with A Chinese Courtesan's Dictionary*, Learner's Bookstore, 1980.

Yalom, Marilyn, *A History of the Breast*, Random House, 1998.

Zapperi, Roberto, *L'homme enceint*, Presses universitaires de France, 1983.

Zelman, Joanna, 'Breast milk cheese available at the lady cheese shop,' *Huffington Post*, 24 May 2011.

Zevit, Ziony, 'The Adam and Eve Story: Eve Came From Where?: Adam and Eve in the Bible', *Bible History Daily* via *Biblical Archaeology*, 11 June 2023.

INDEX